SKIN CANVAS DESIGNS

SAVAGE TATTOOS:

A NATURE AND ANIMAL COLORING BOOK

 **KATE TAYLOR DESIGN**

This book features 40 intricate illustrations. Each illustration is printed on one side of the page, providing a convenient and enjoyable coloring experience for adults.

SCAN ME

Scan this QR code to visit our Amazon page, and if you enjoy this coloring book, please consider leaving a positive review to support our work.

Thank you!

SAVAGE TATTOOS

A Nature and Animal Coloring Book" welcomes you to explore the intricate tattoo designs inspired by the beauty and ferocity of the natural world. Unleash your creativity as you color captivating illustrations showcasing the stunning artistry of flora and fauna tattoos. With each page, encounter majestic animals and delicate plants that will spark your imagination and ignite your artistic spirit. Ideal for both beginners and experienced colorists, this collection offers an enchanting and relaxing journey into the untamed beauty of nature and animal-themed tattoos. Embrace your wild side and let your creativity flow with Savage Tattoos!

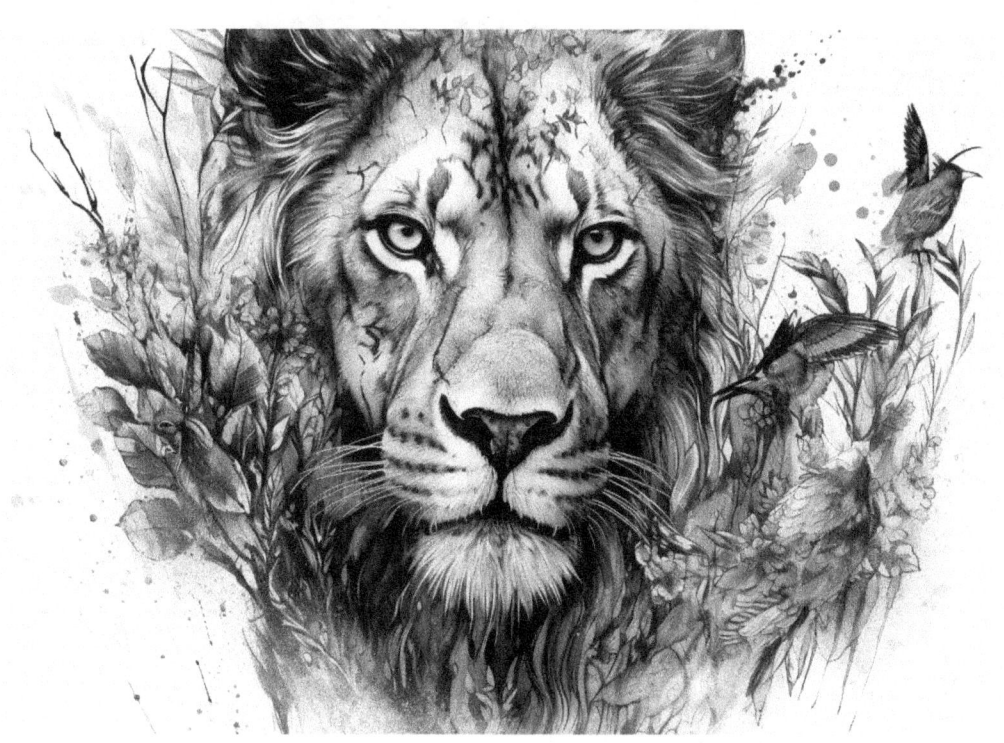

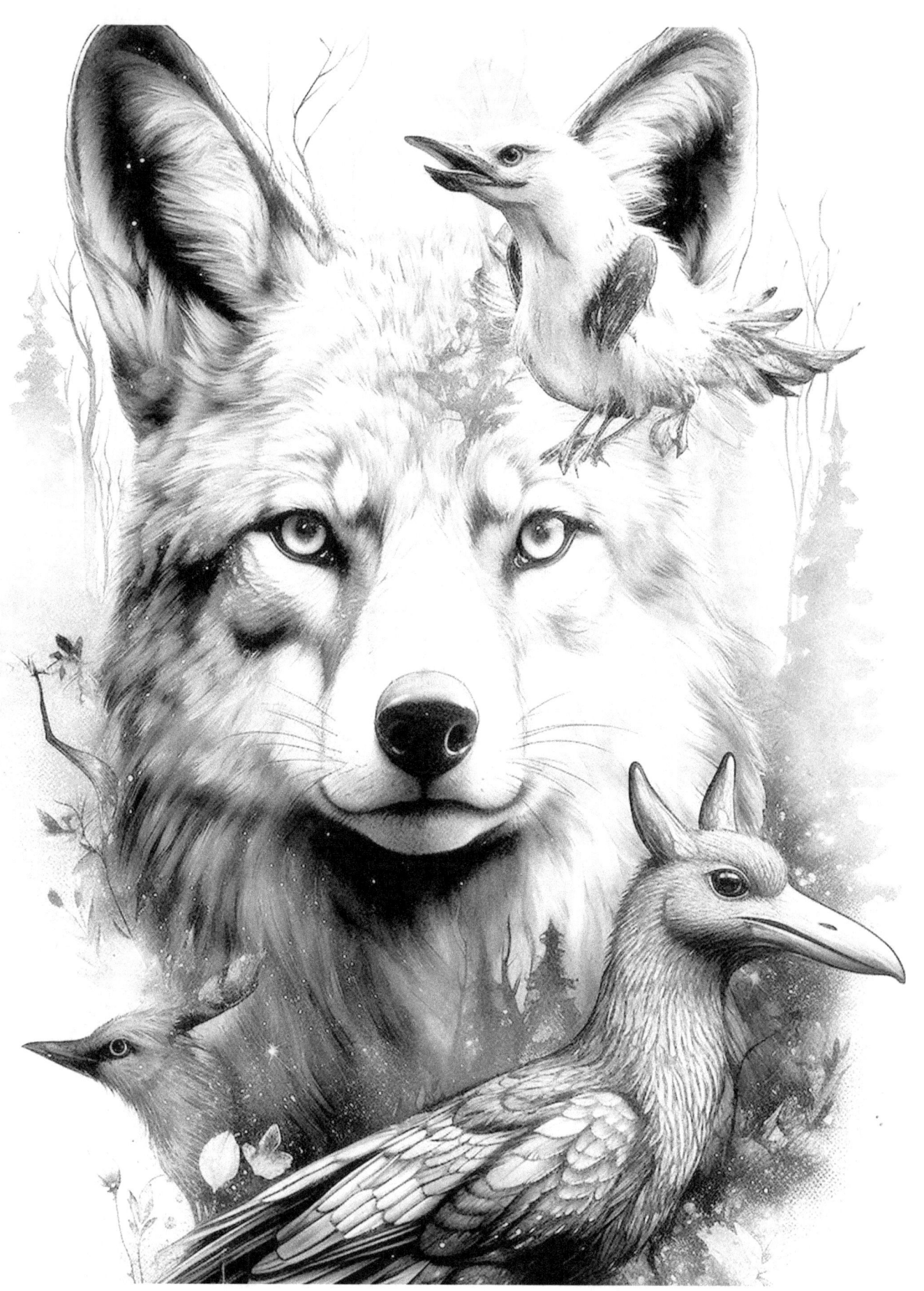

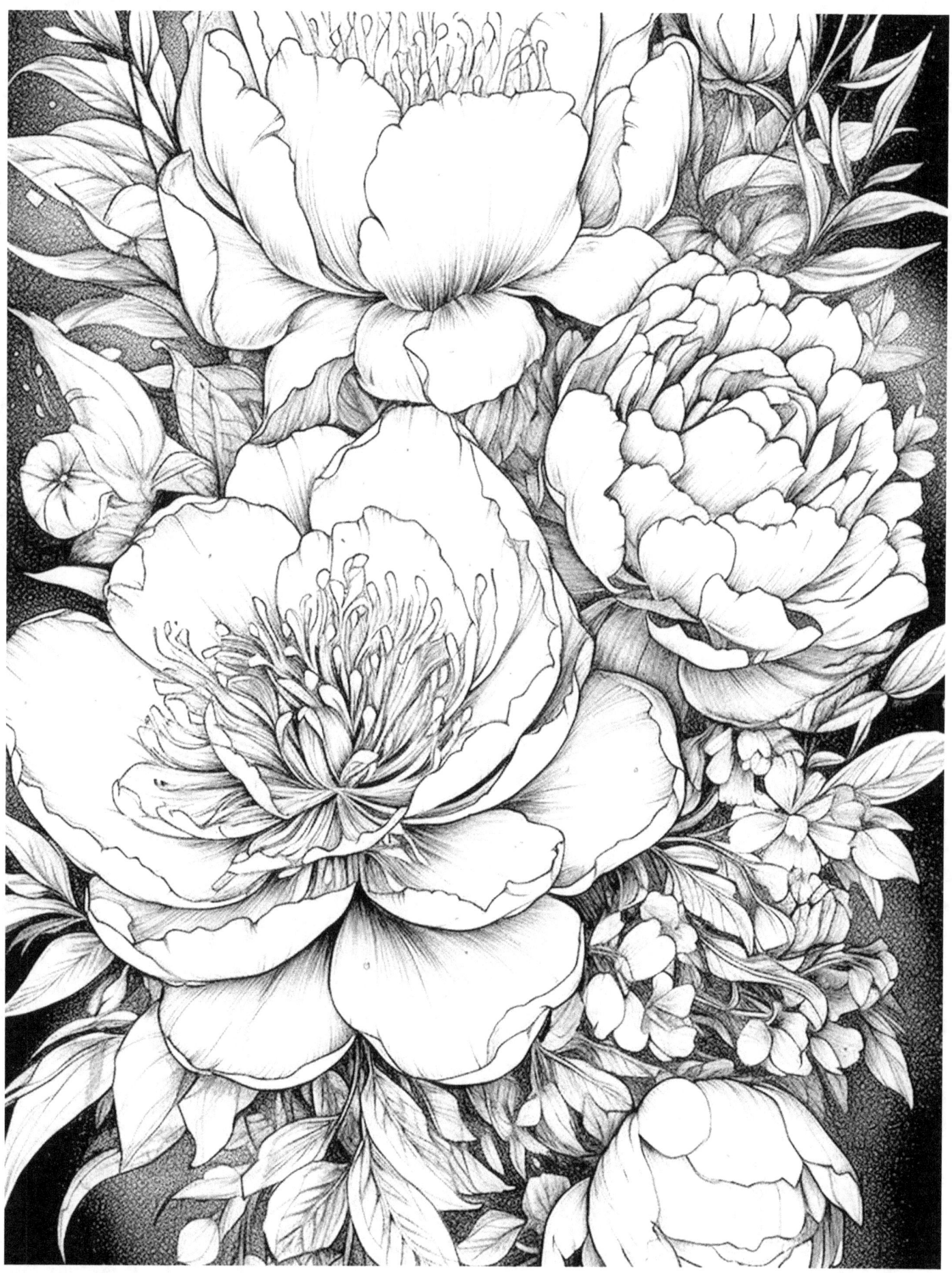

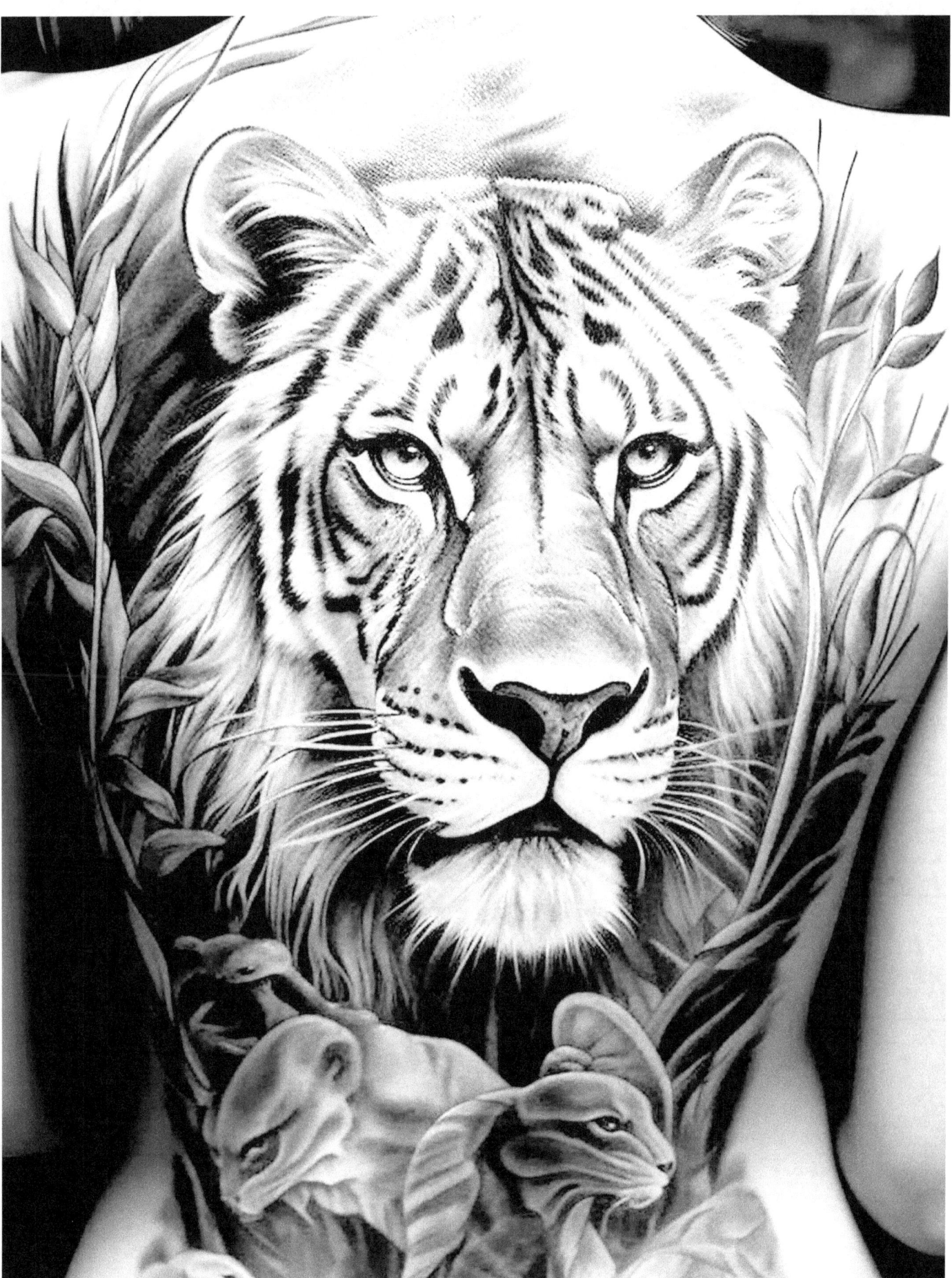

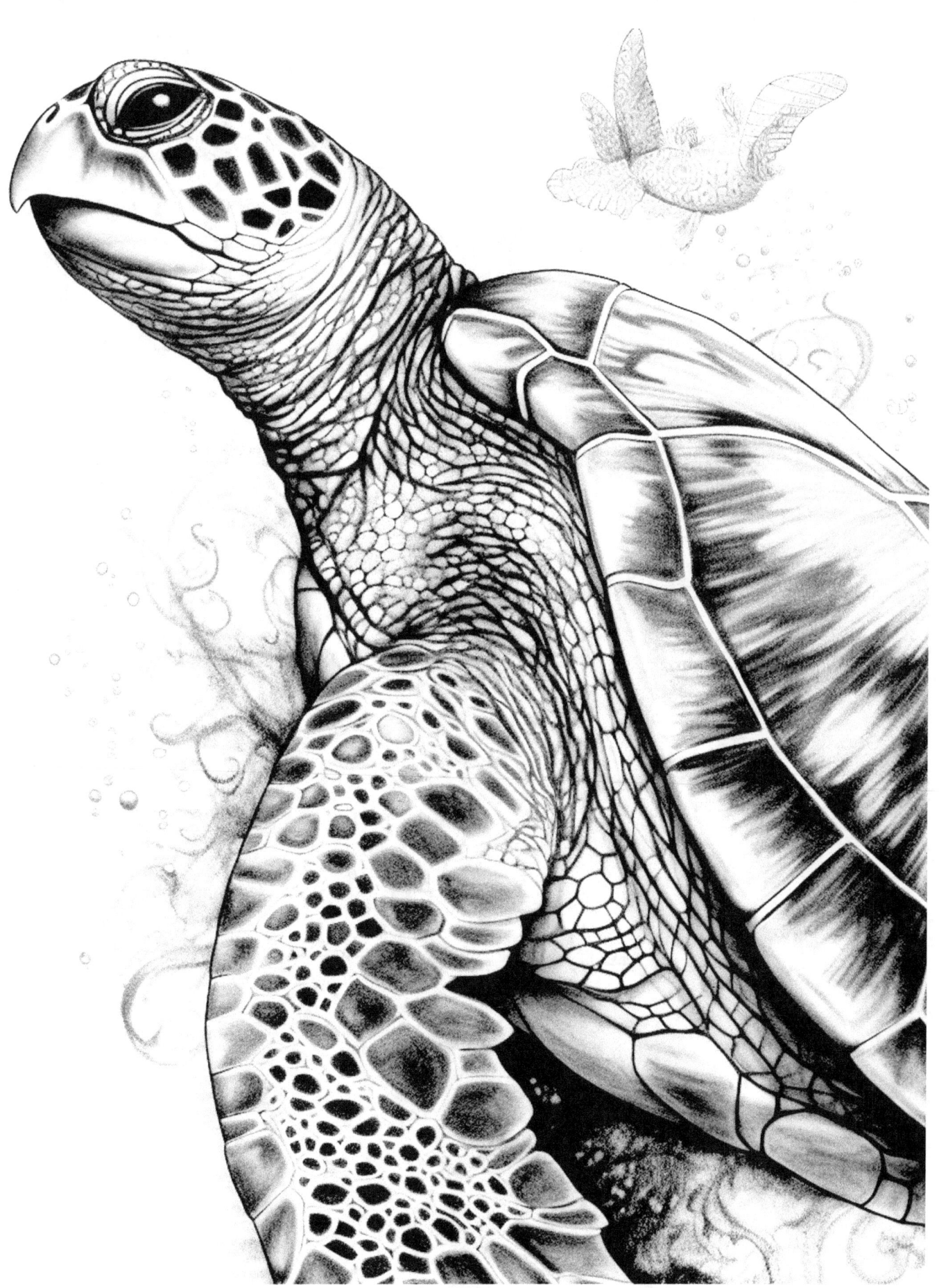

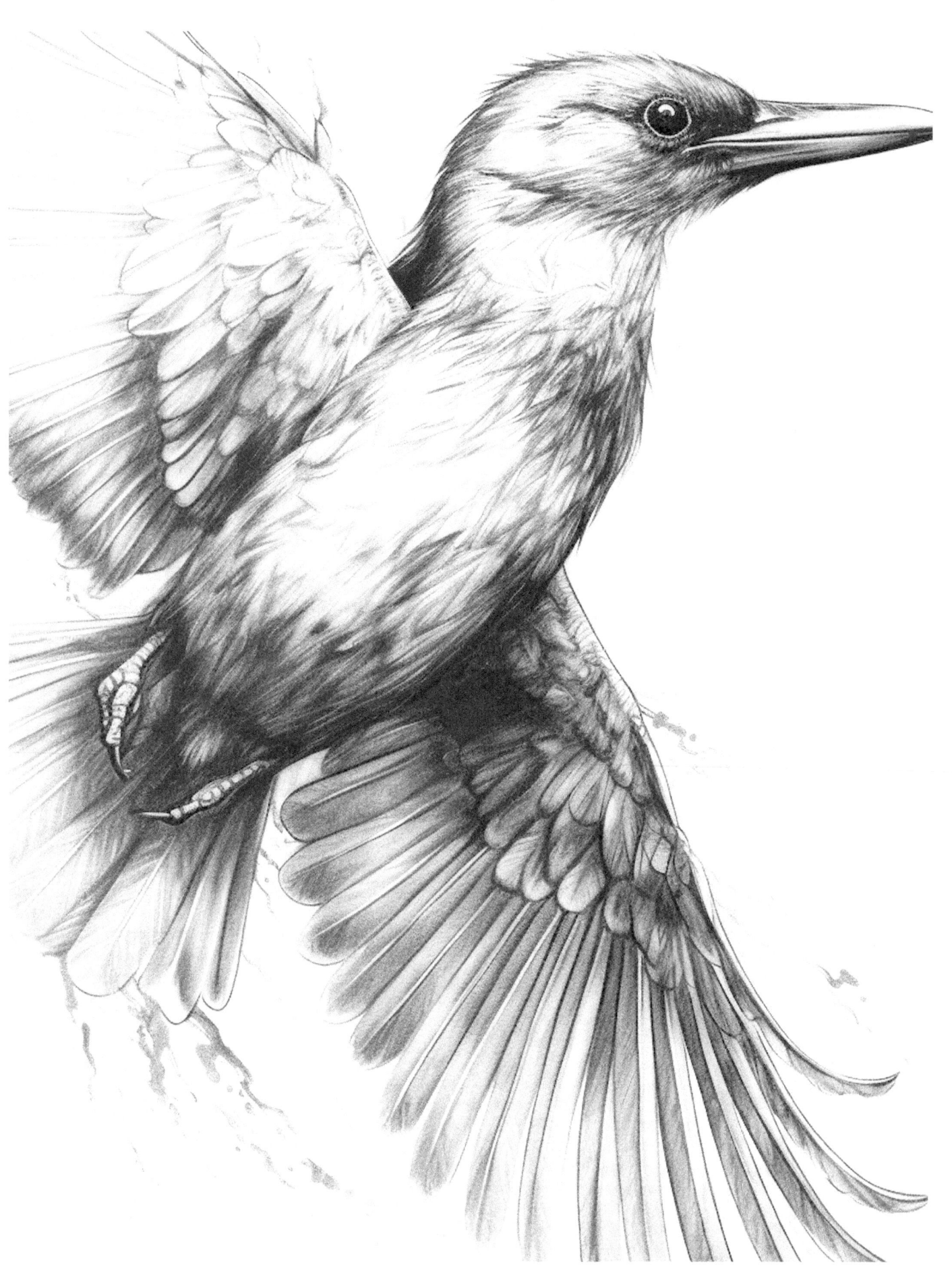

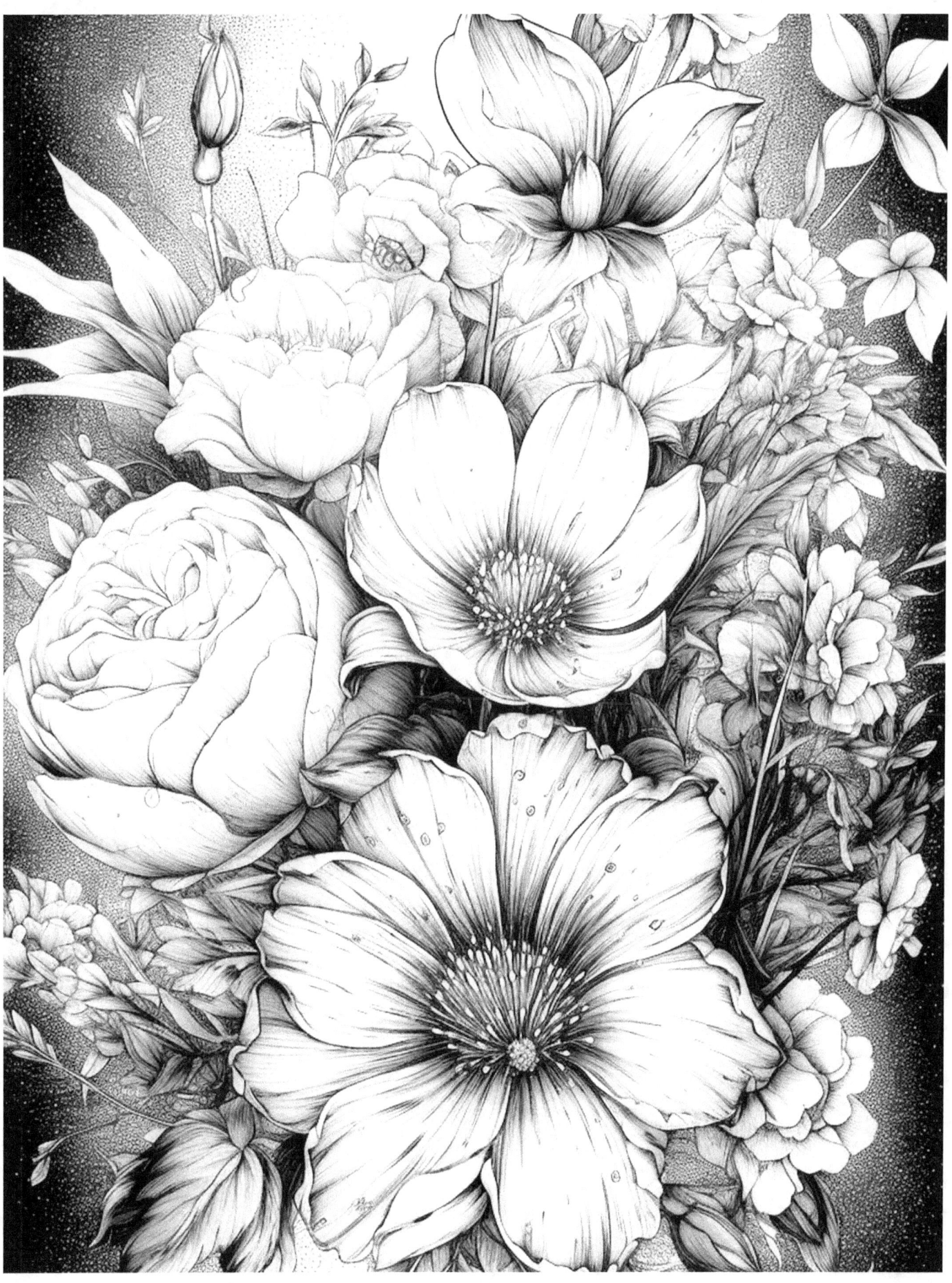

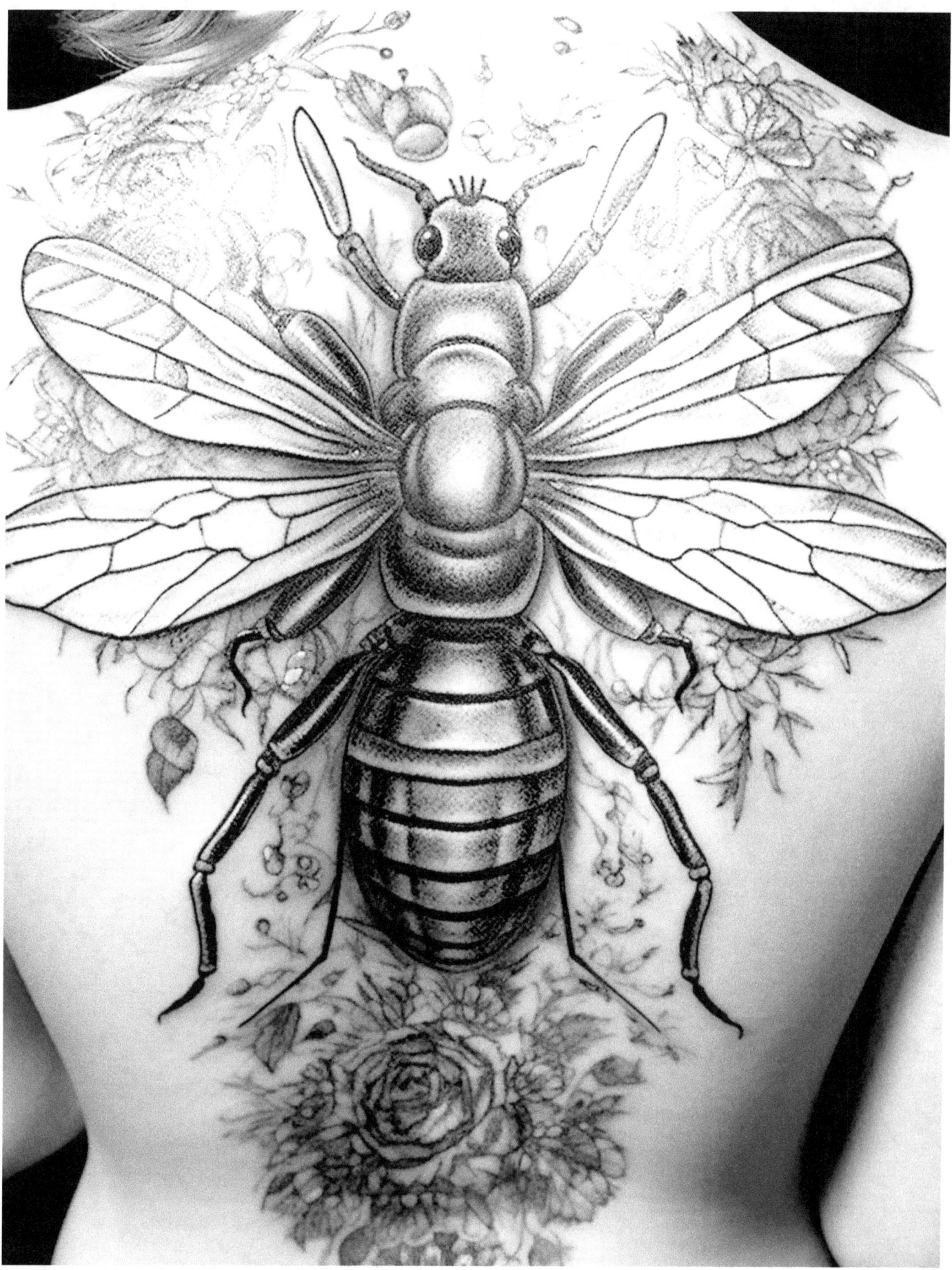

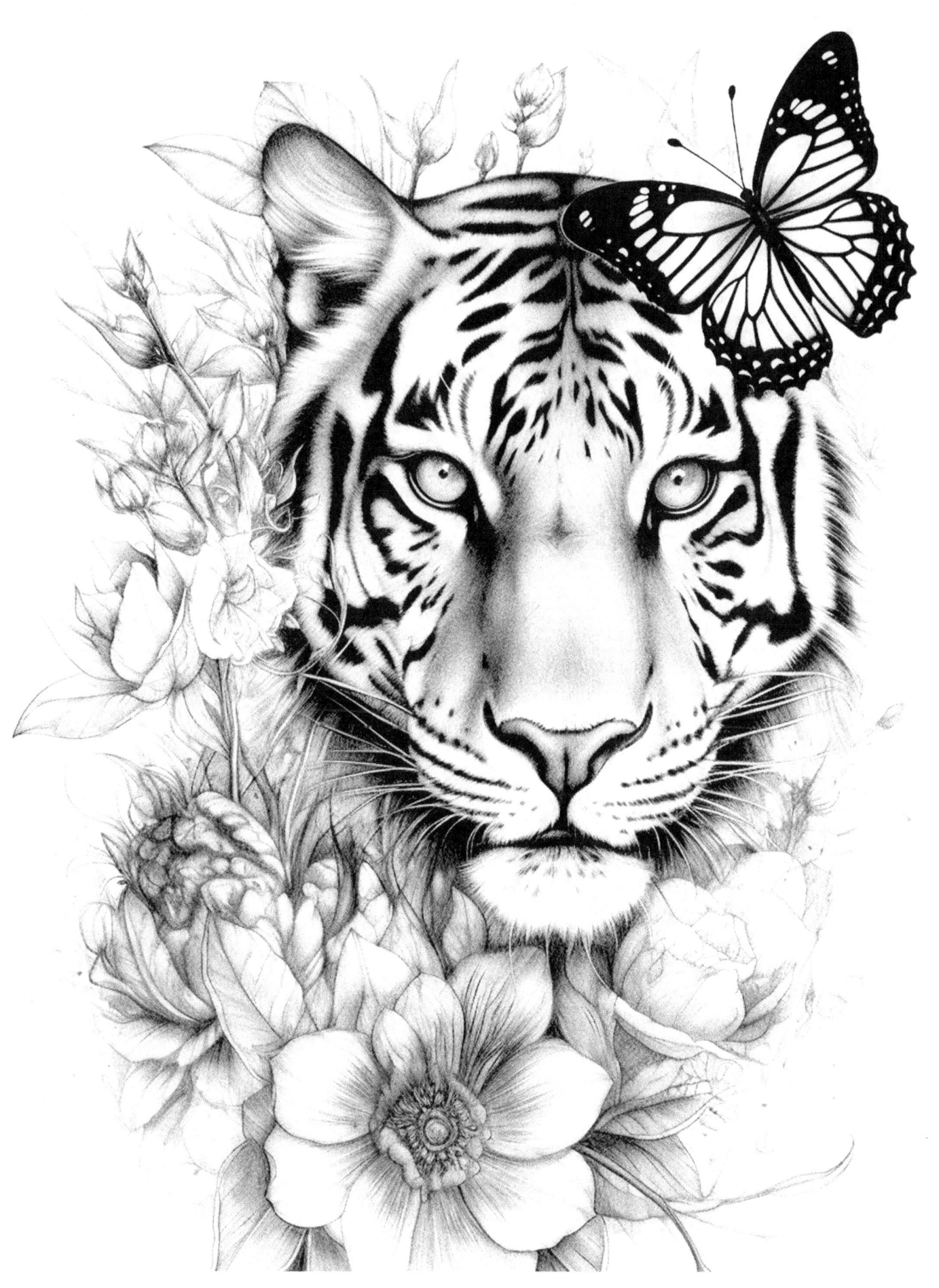

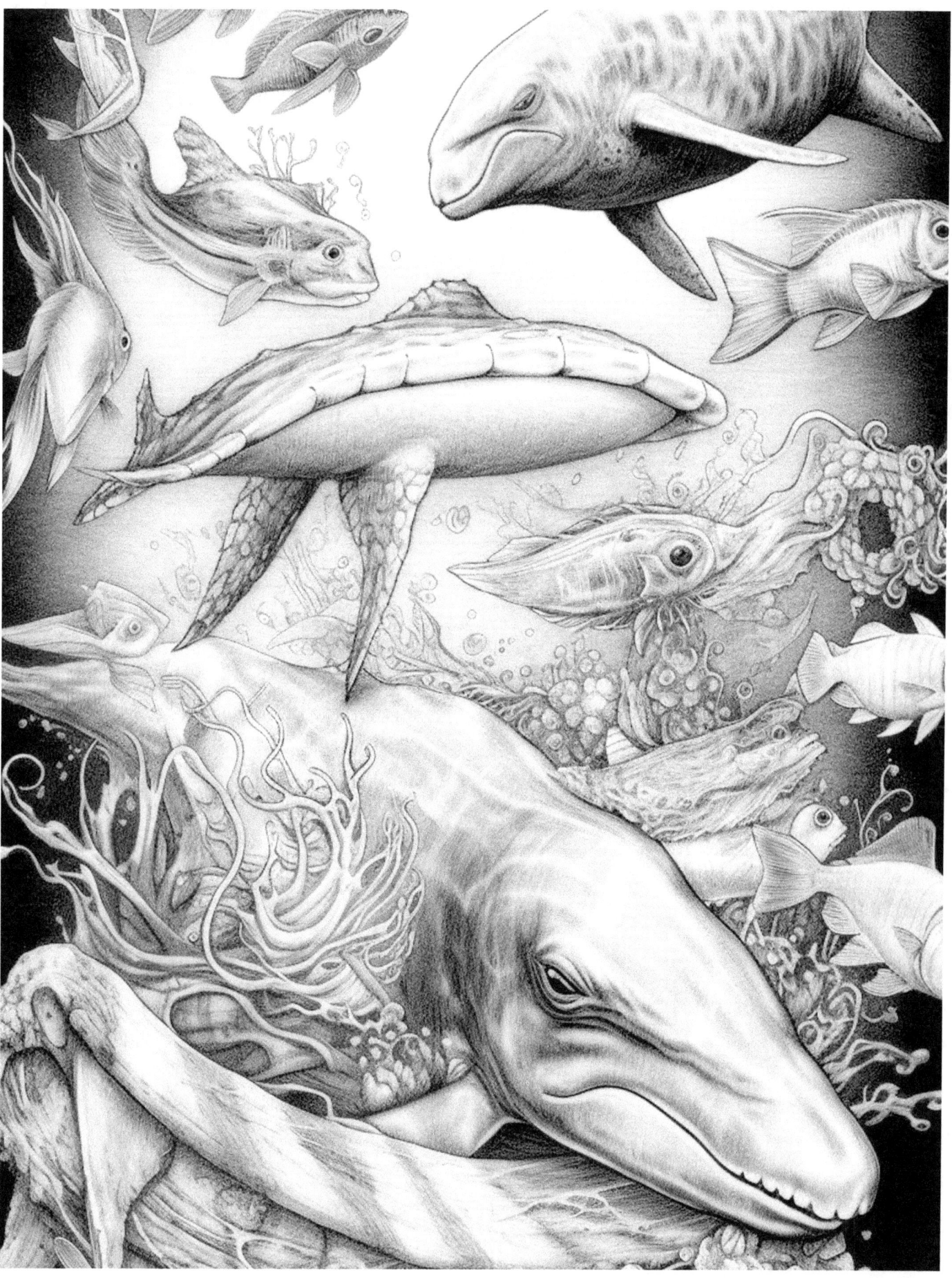

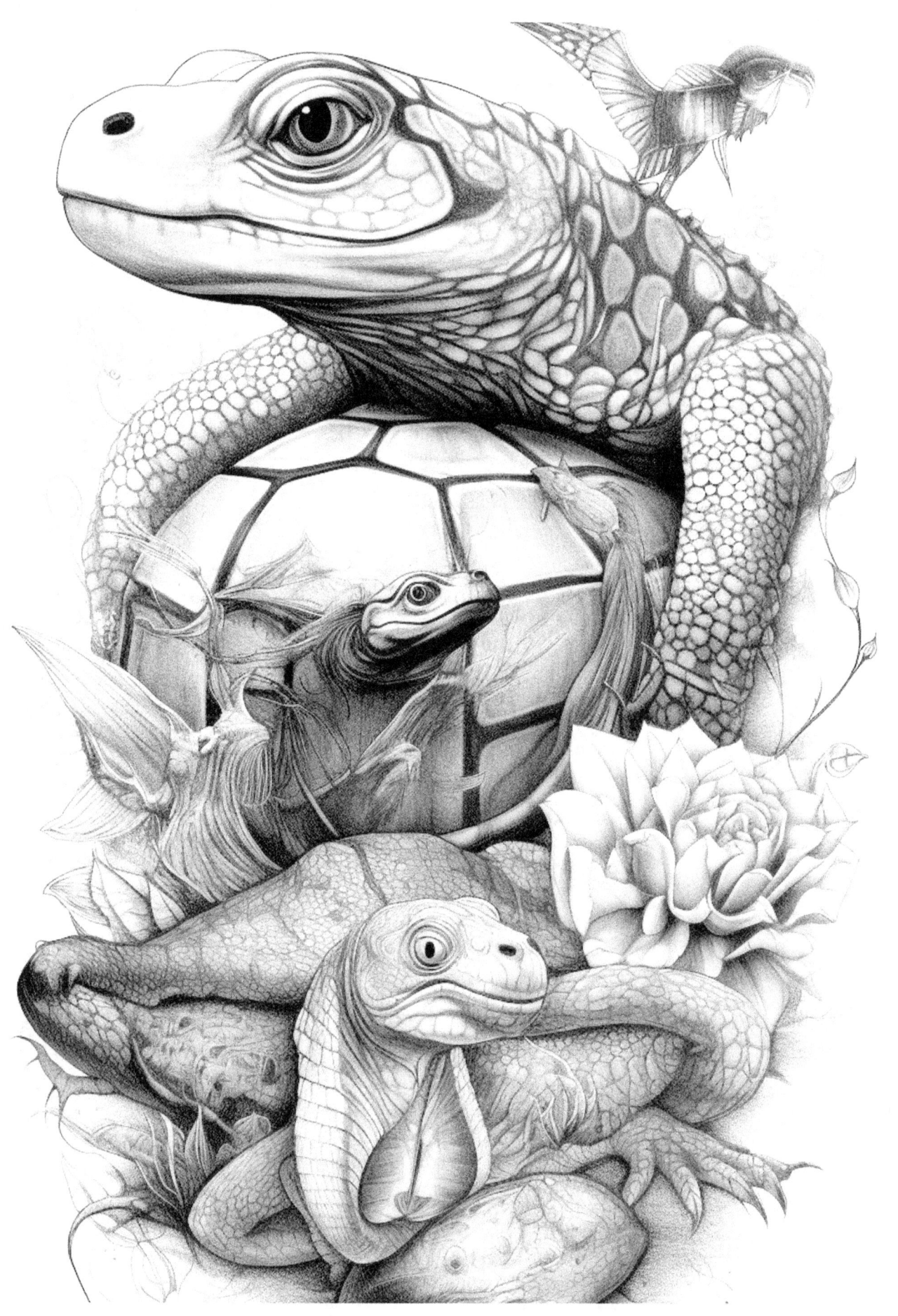

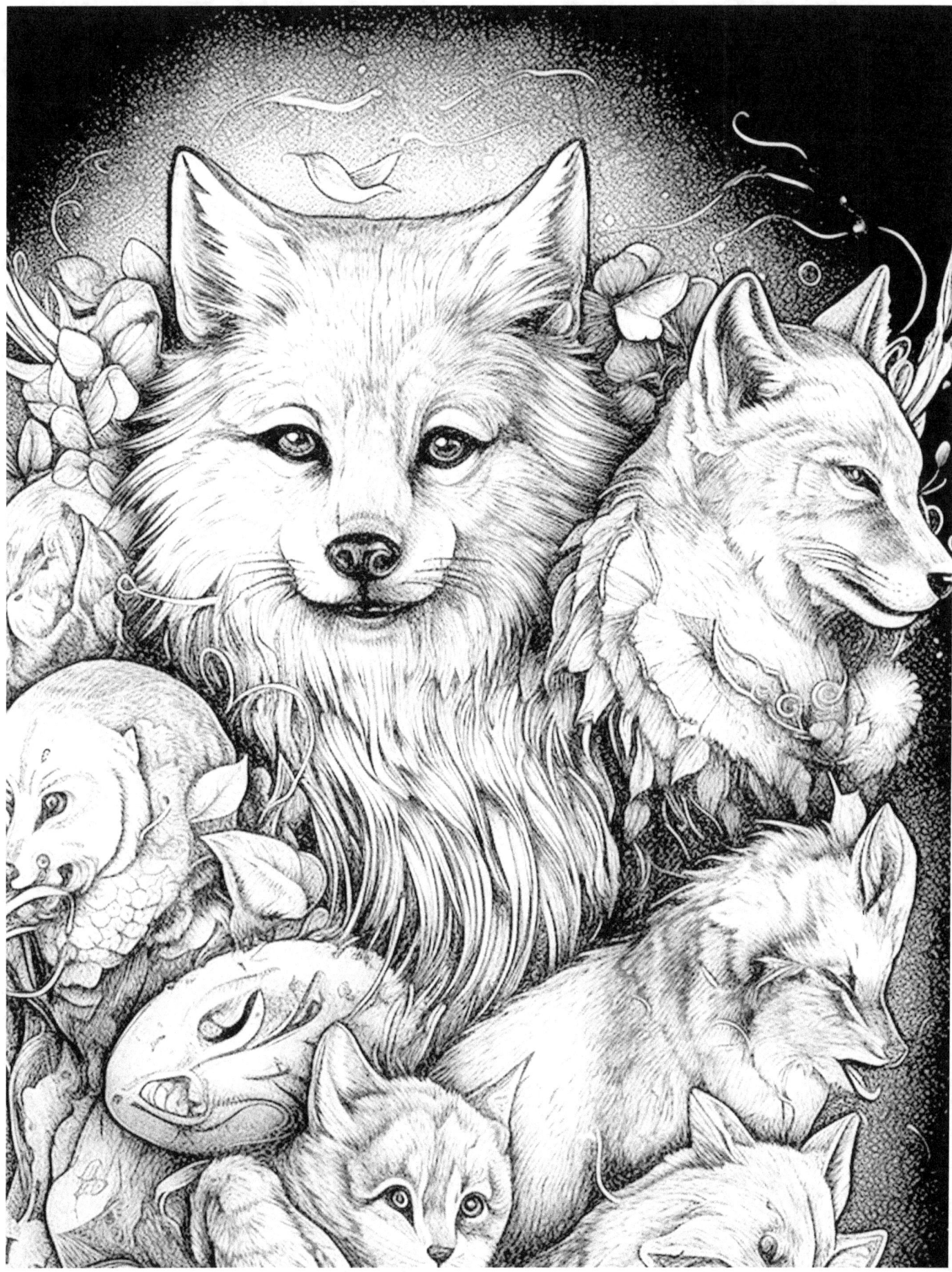

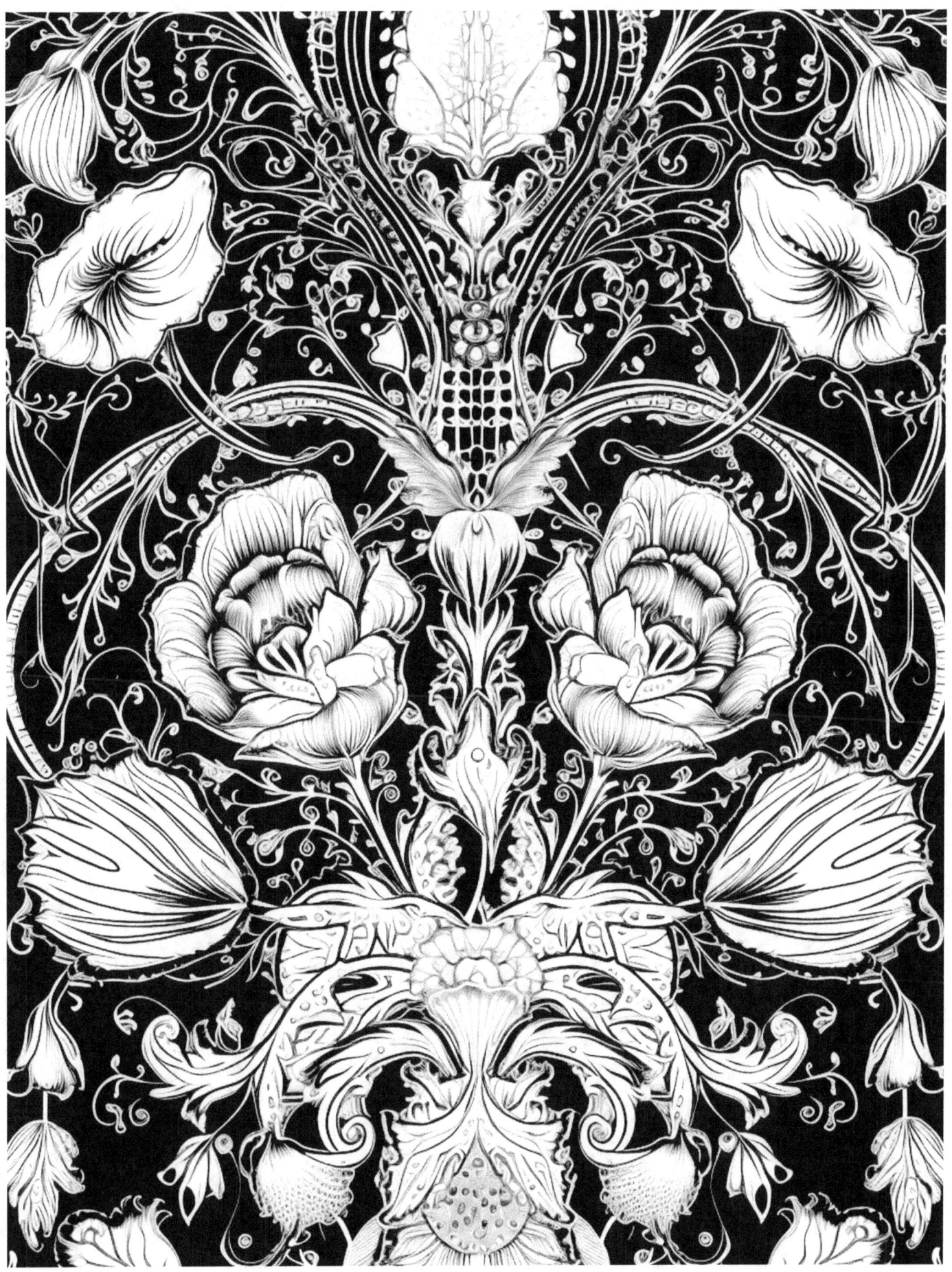

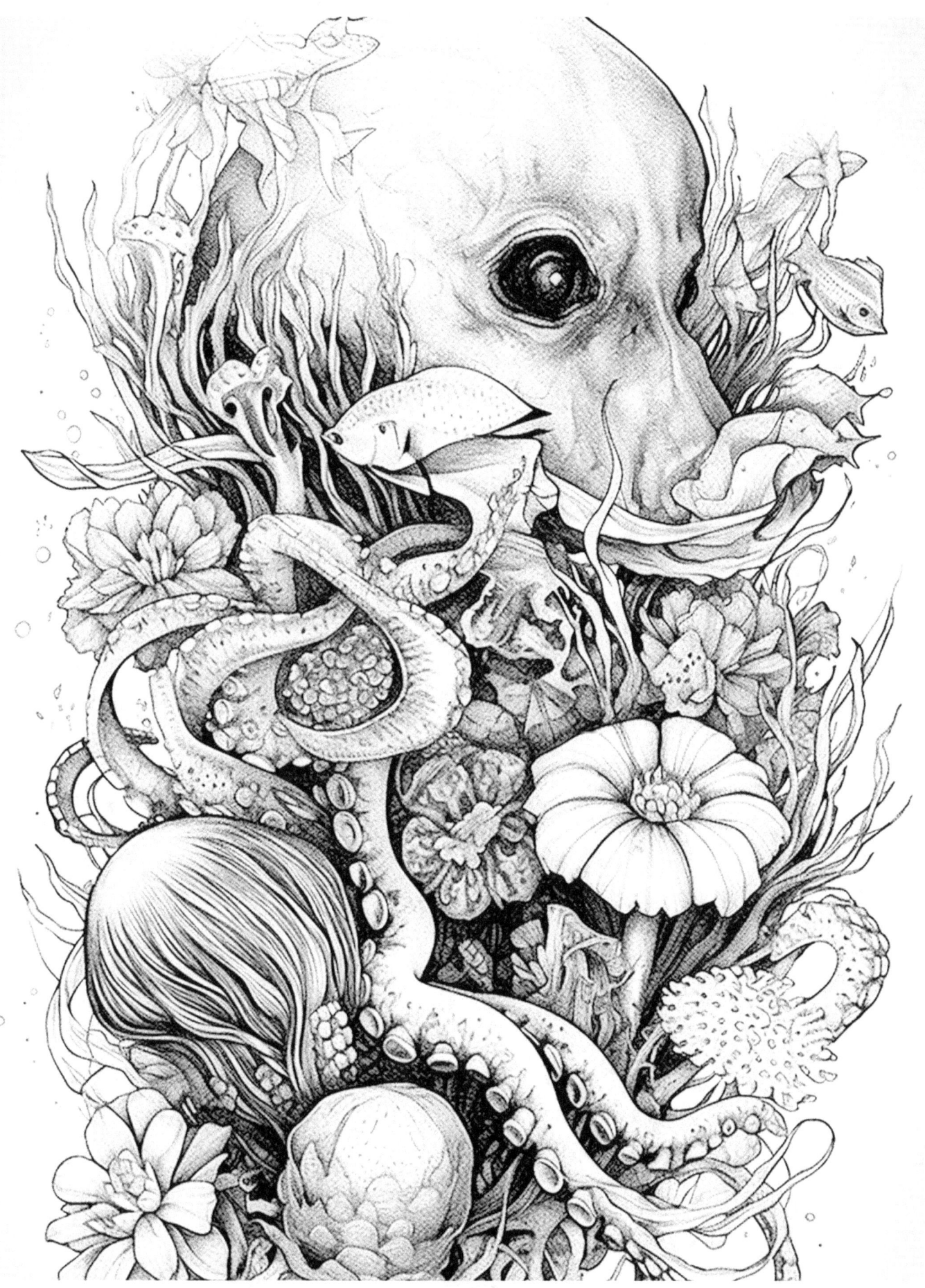

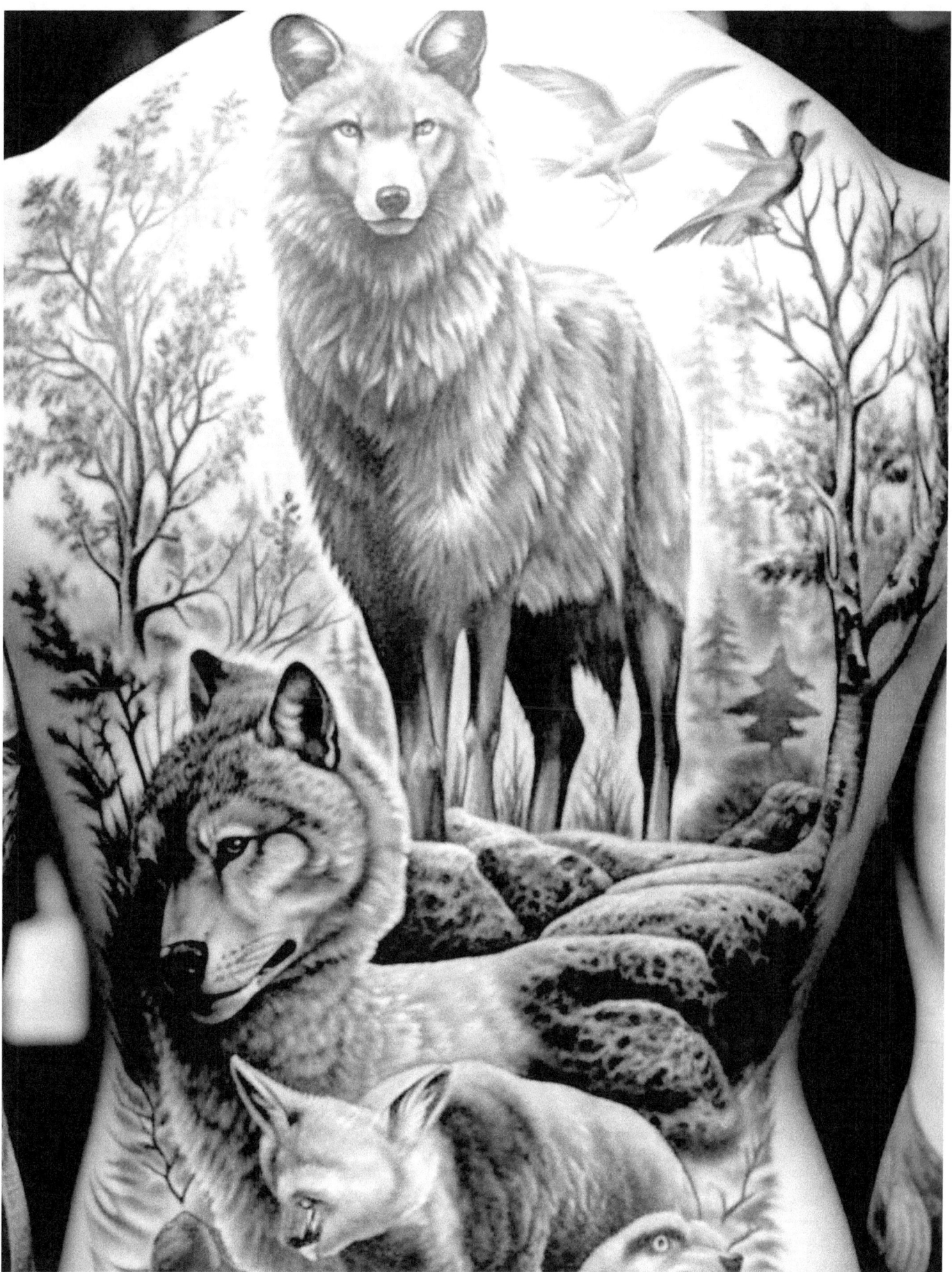

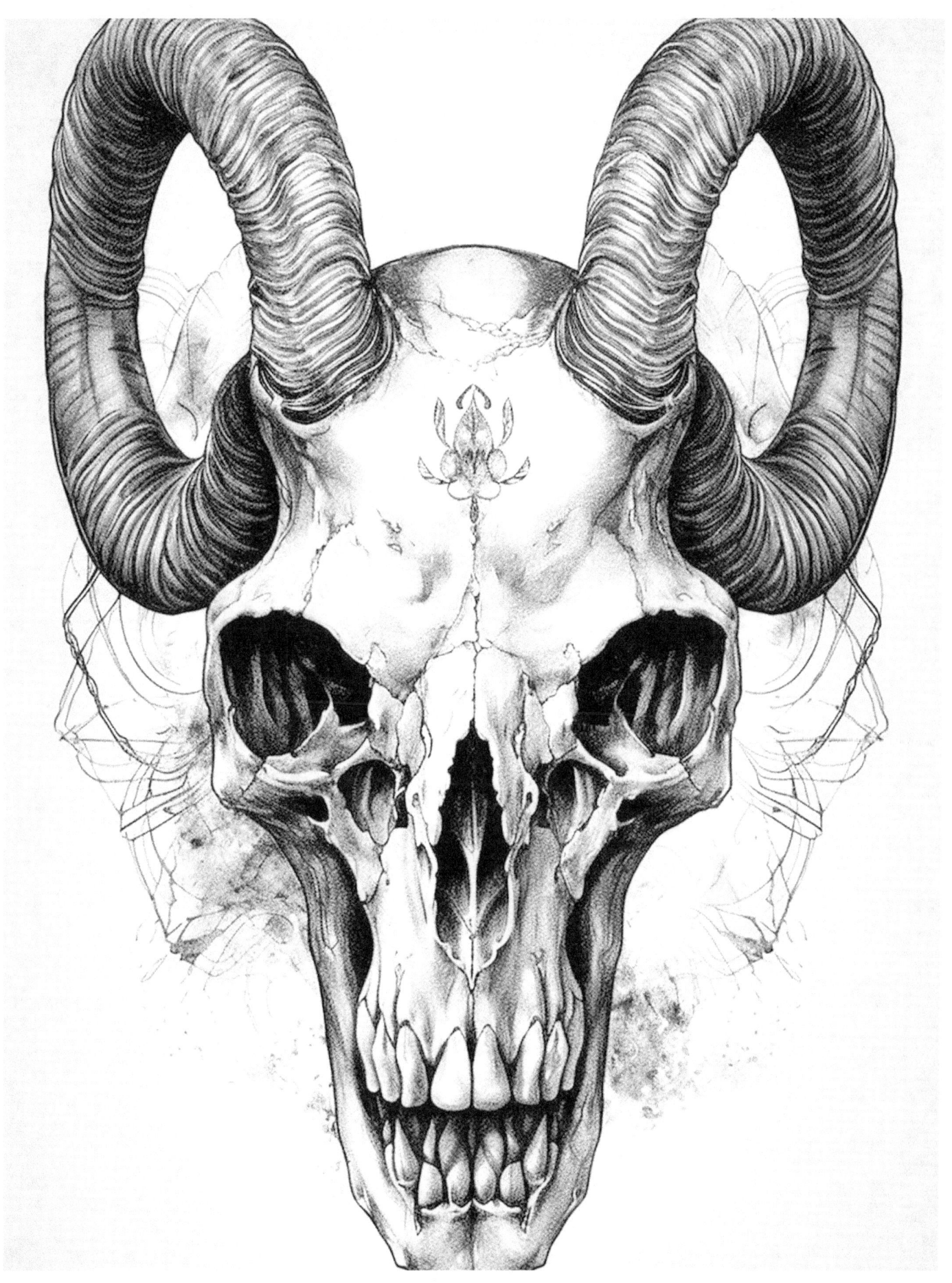

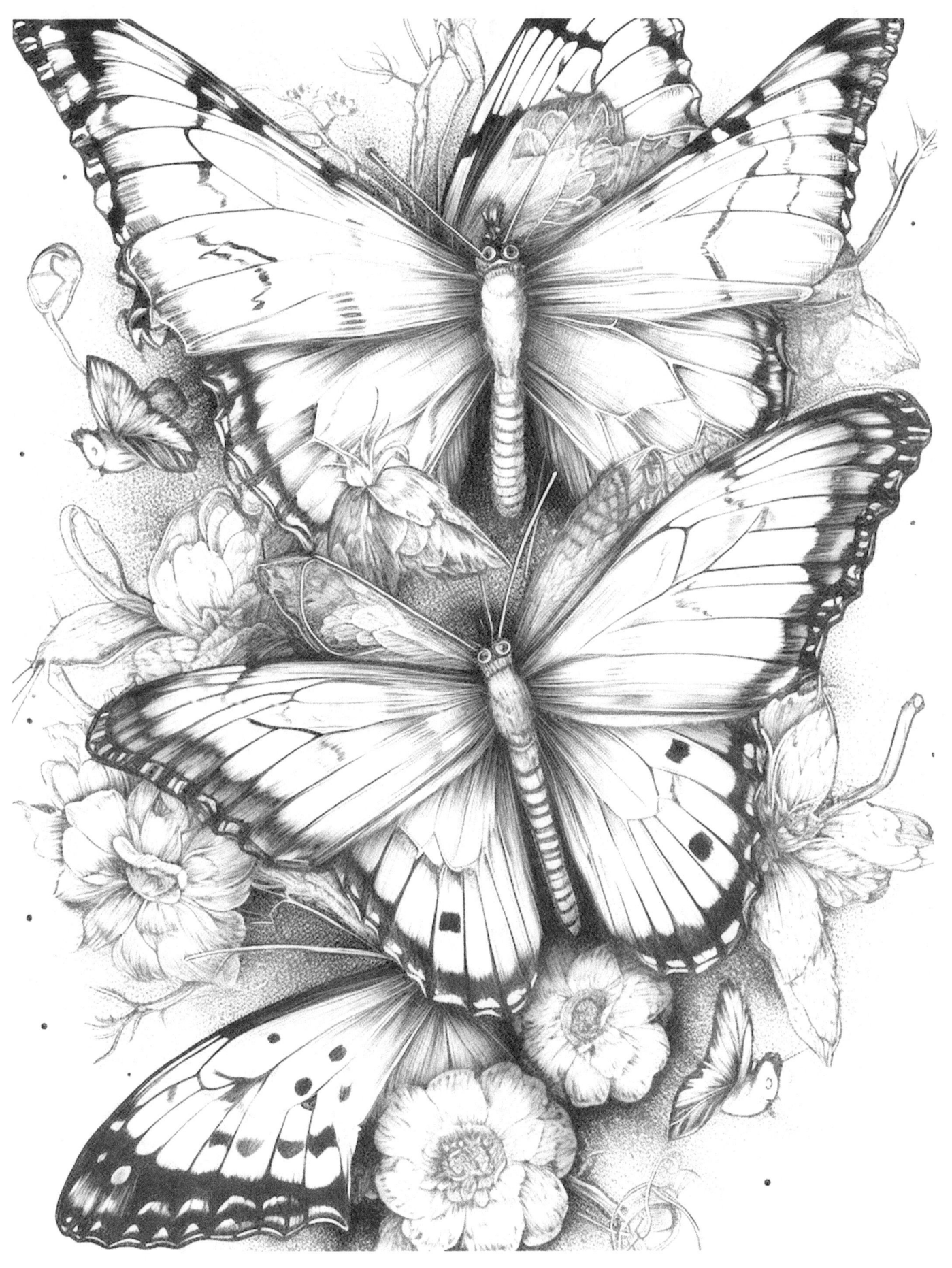

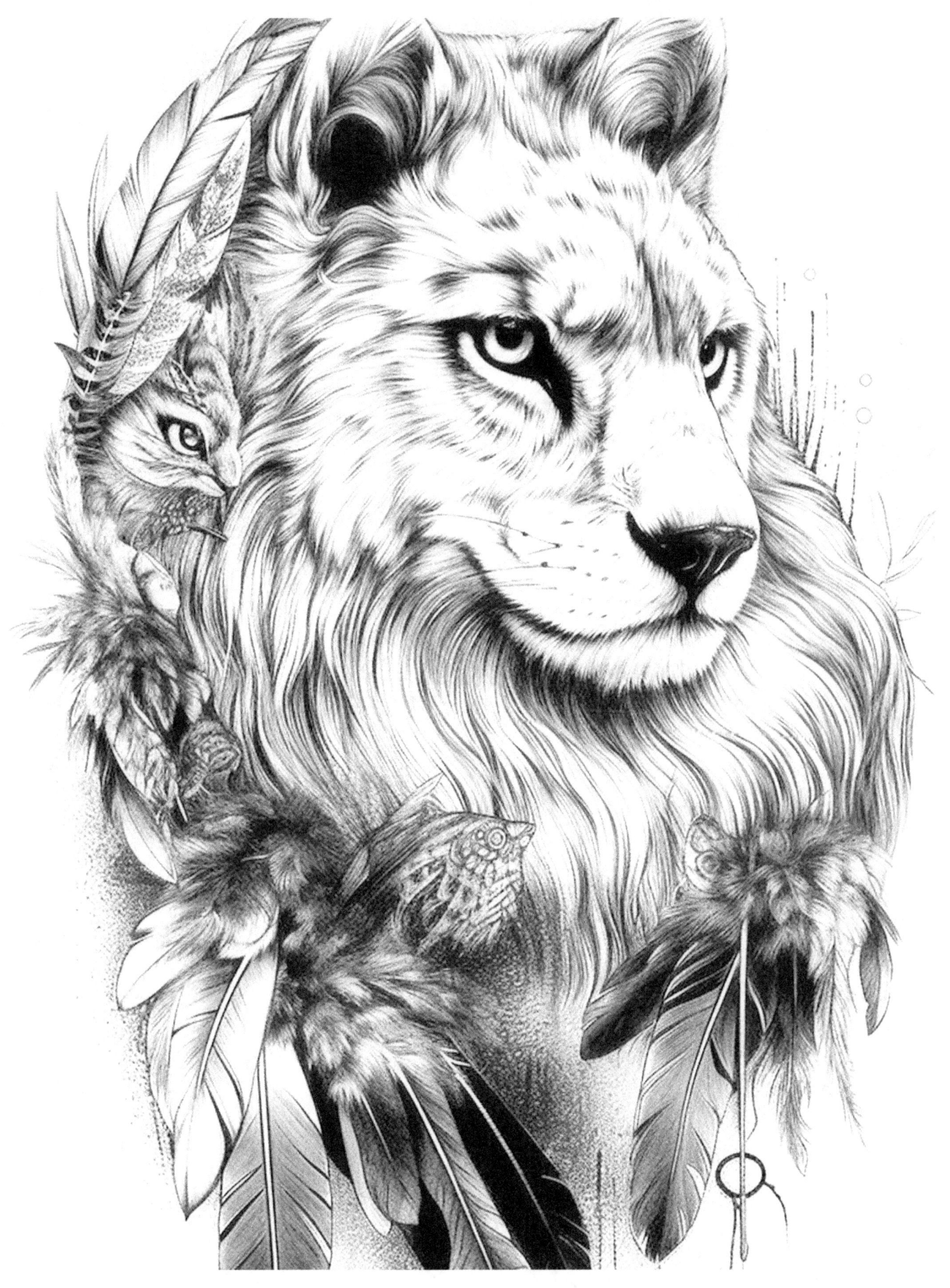

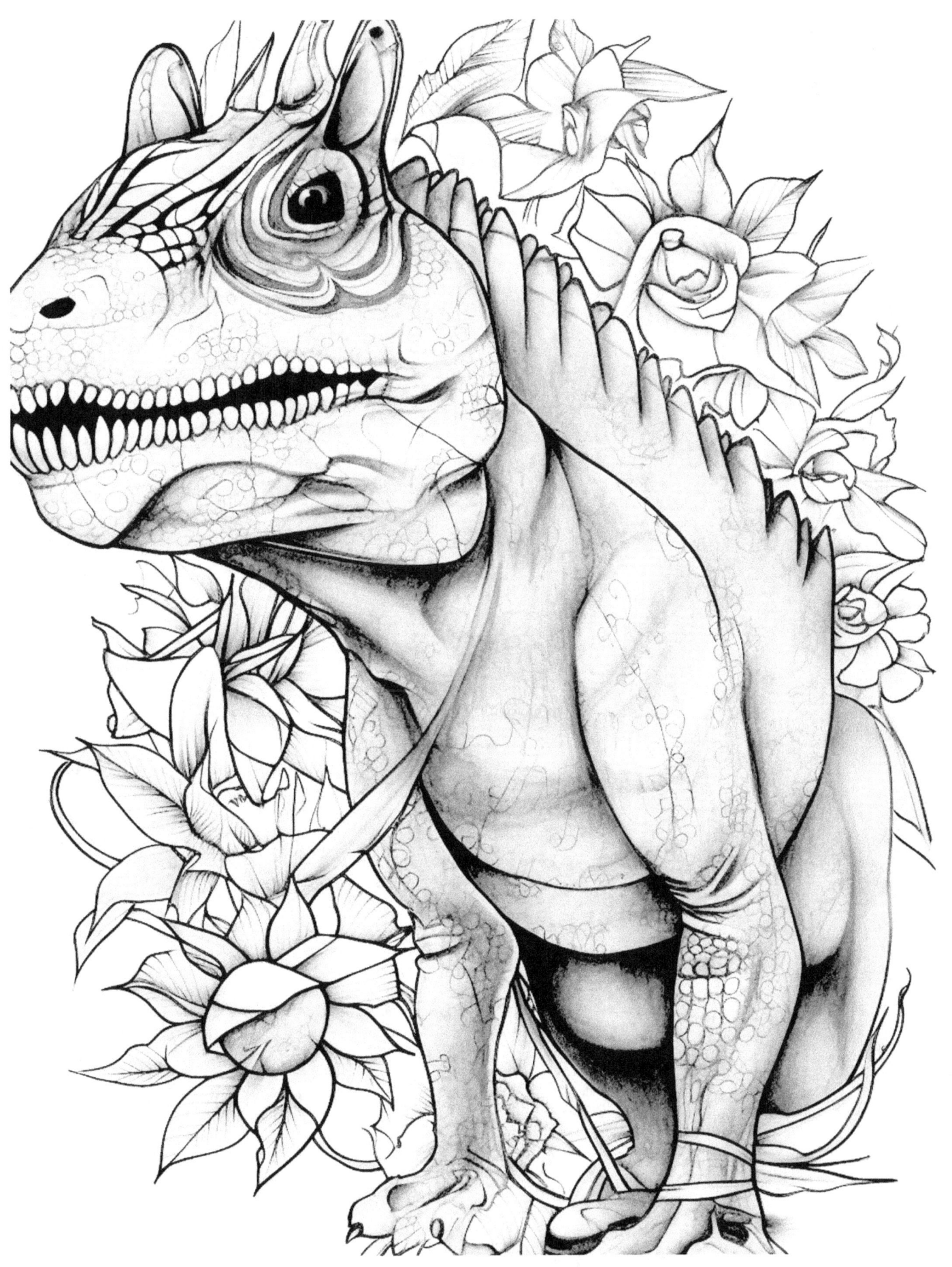

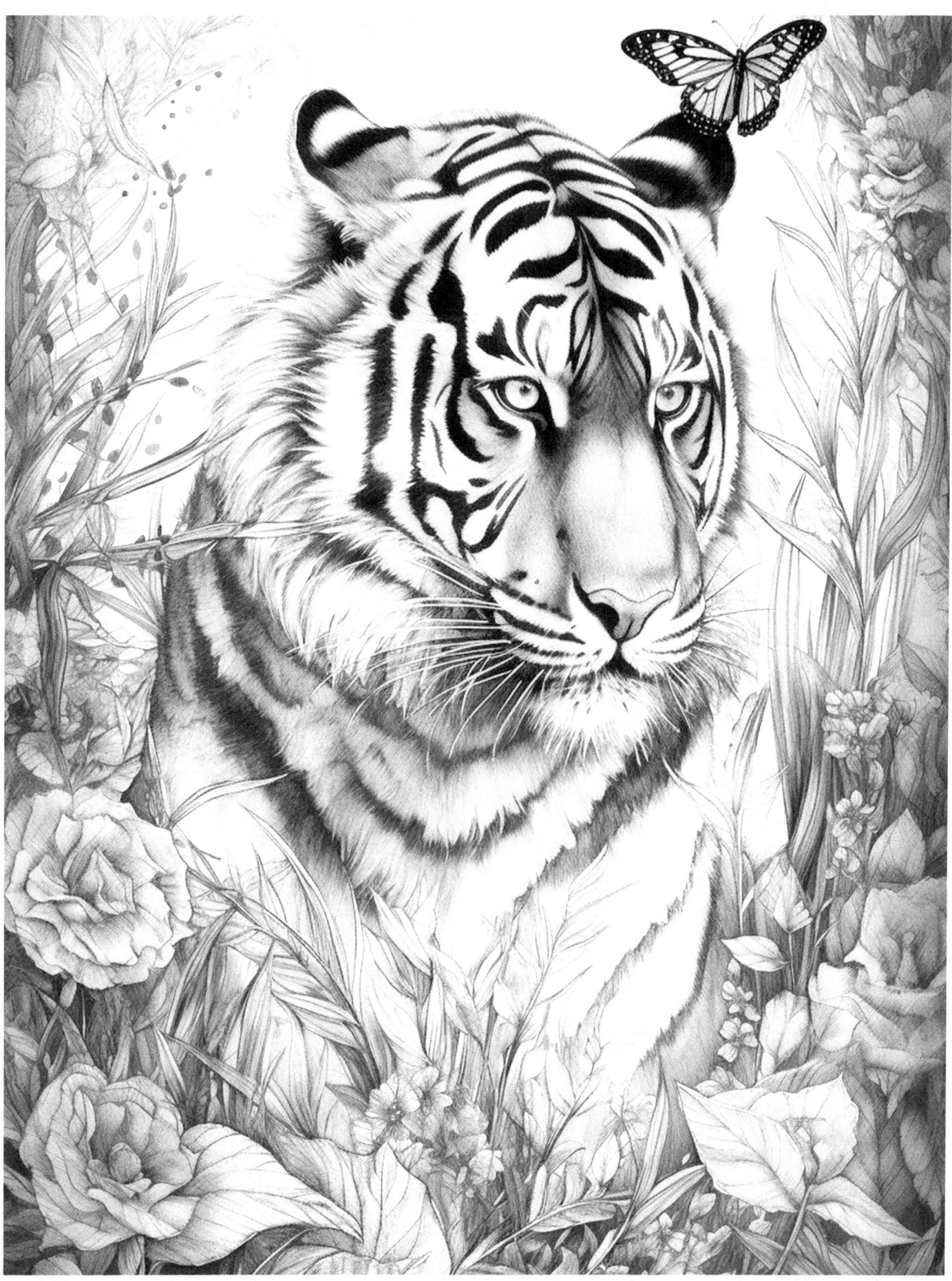

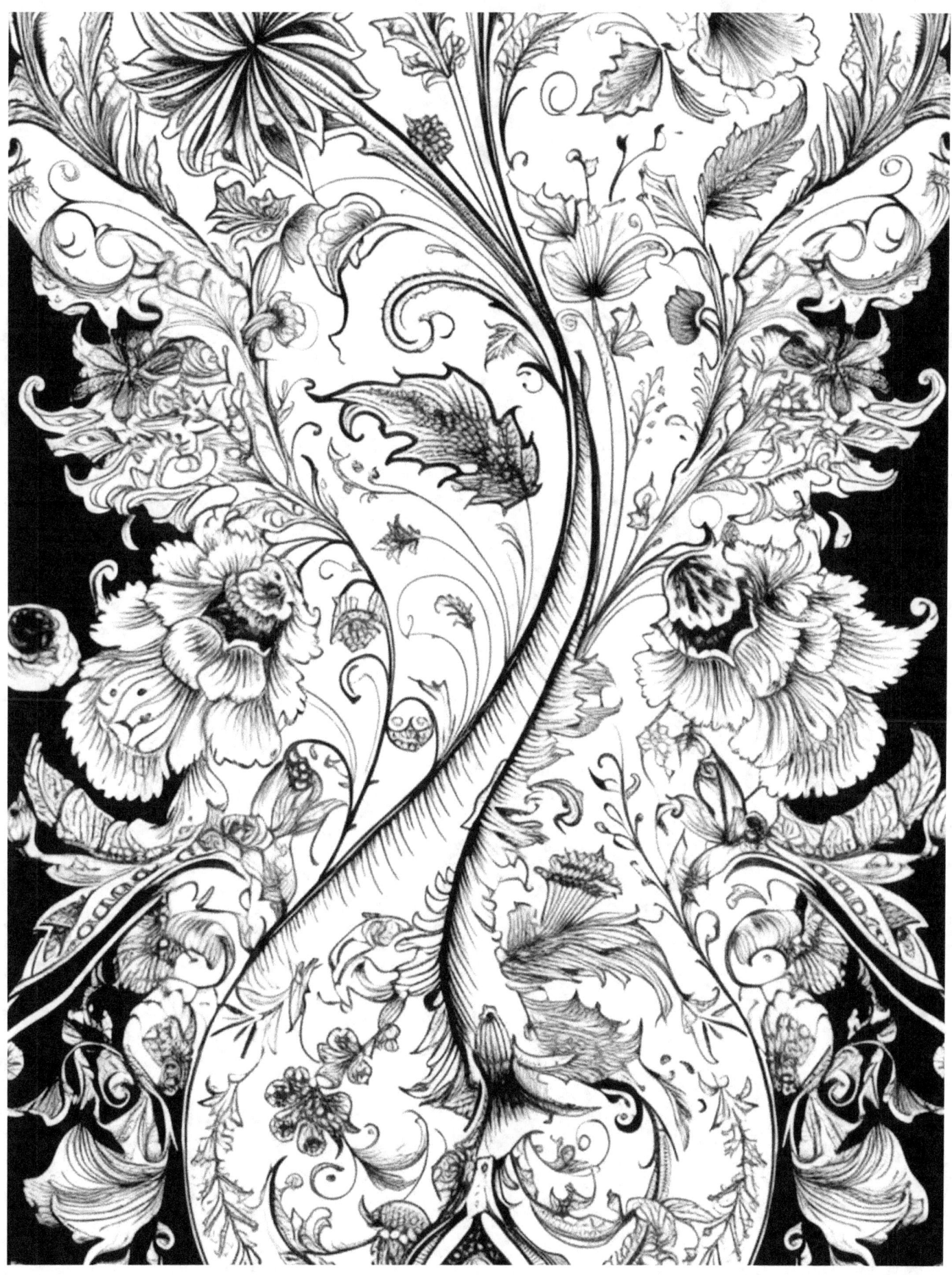

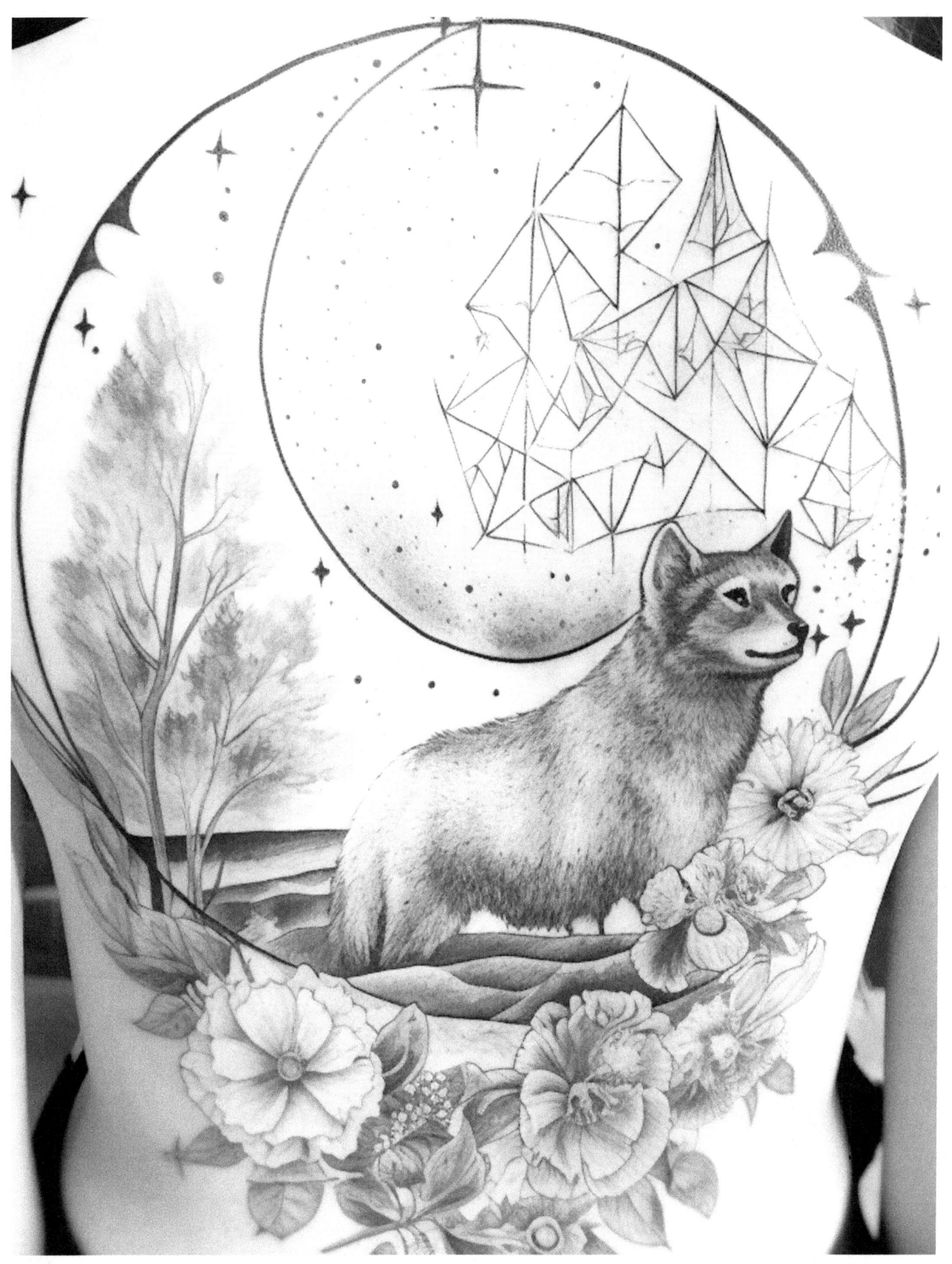

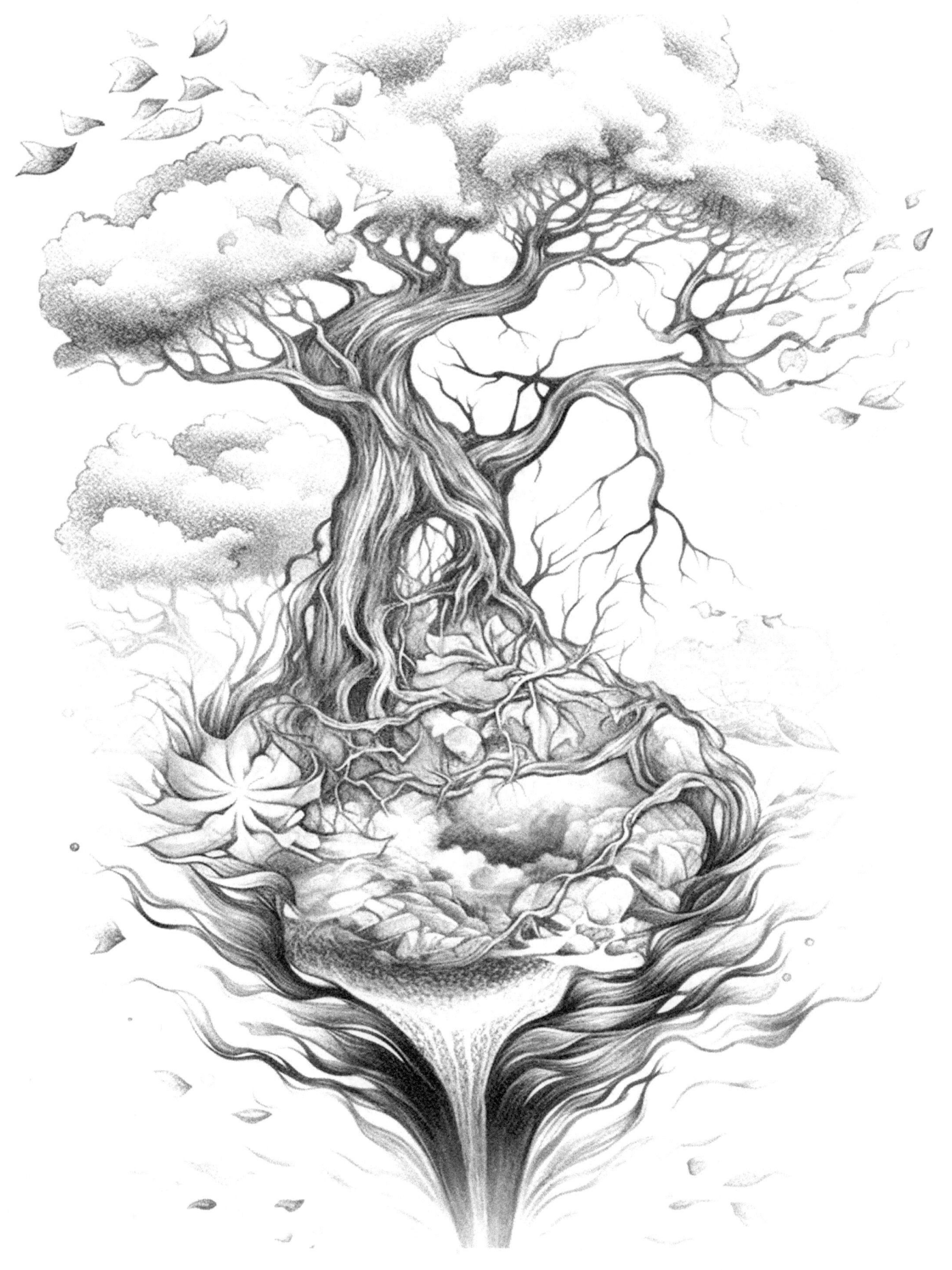

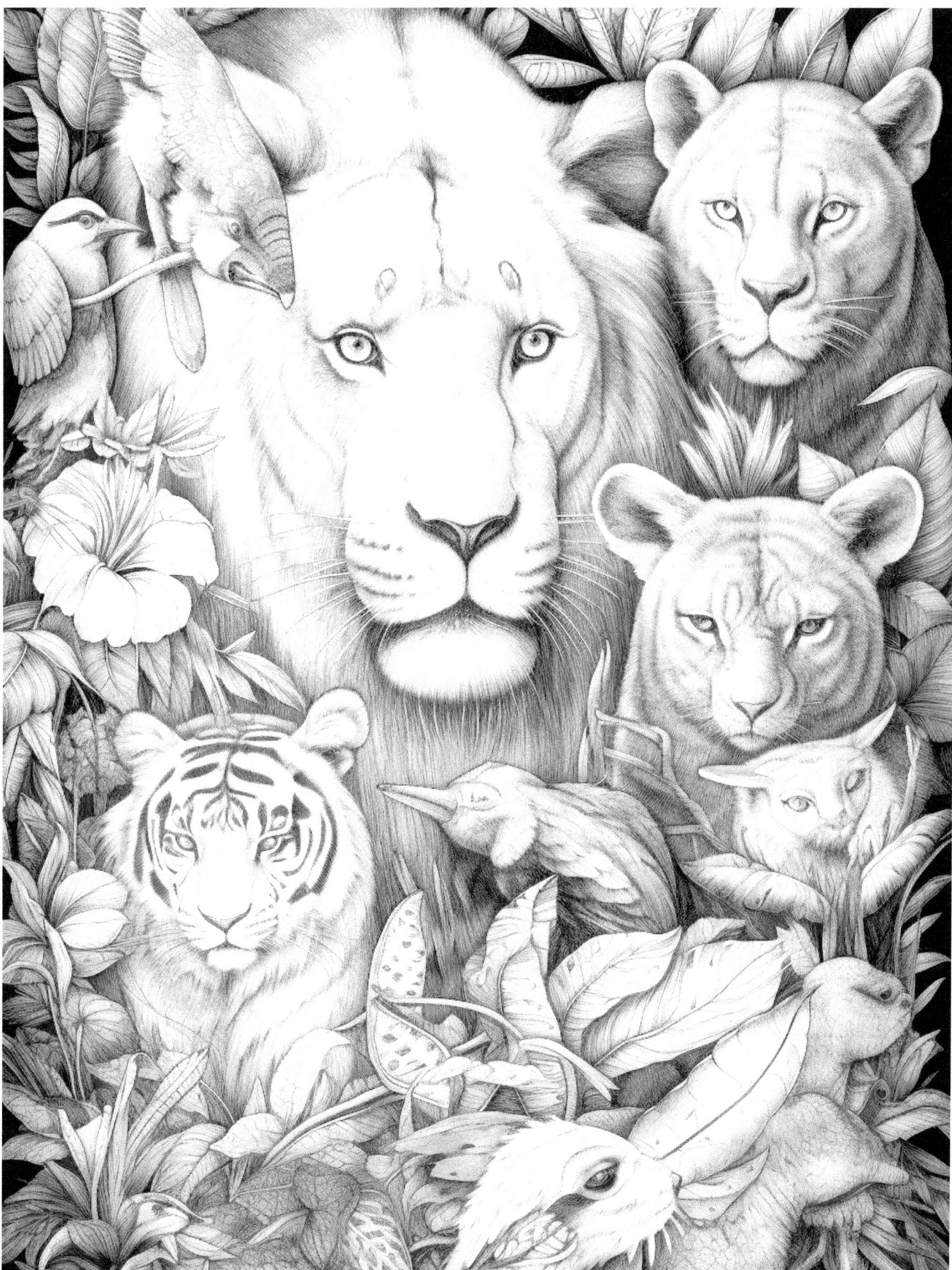

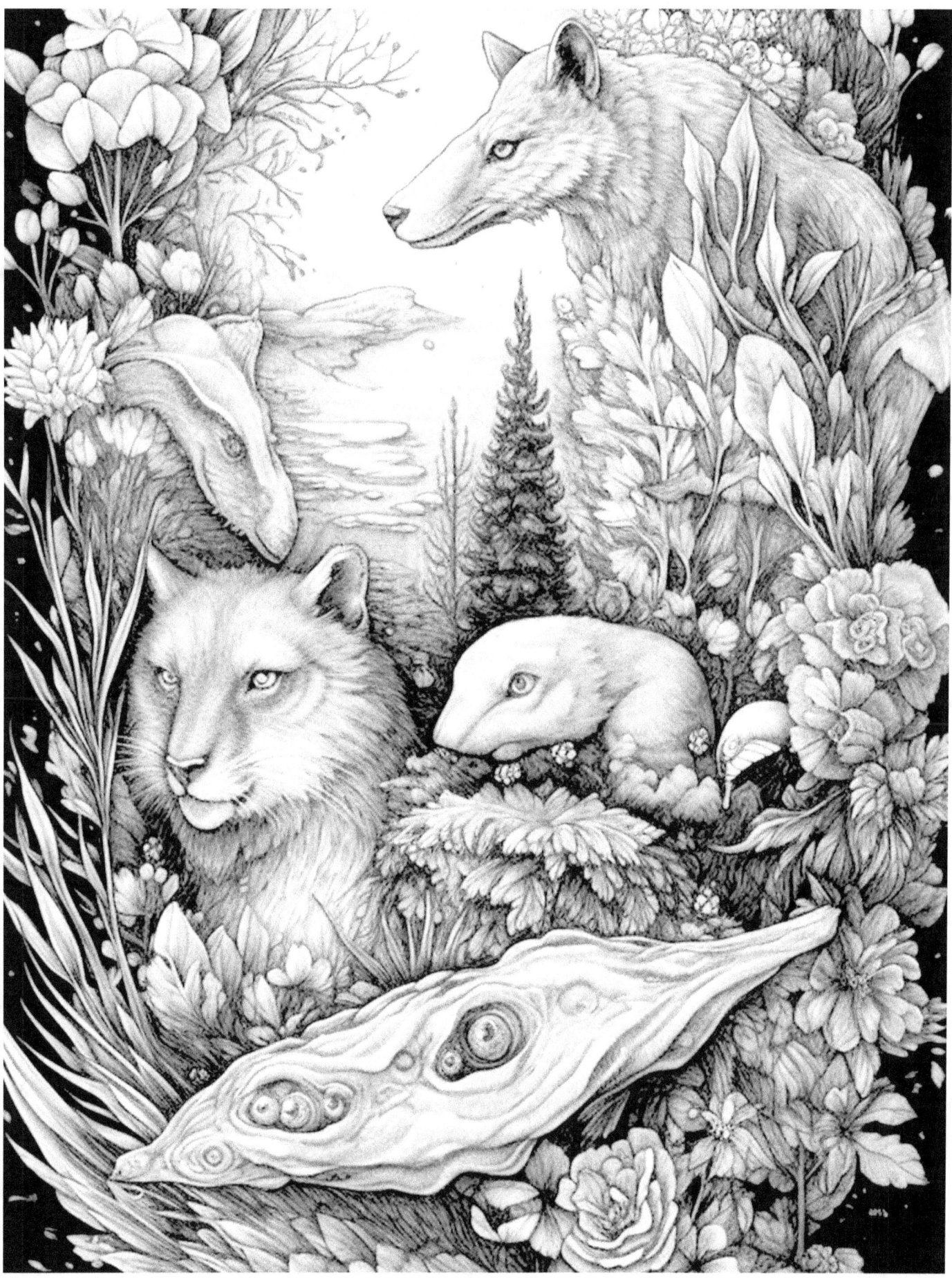

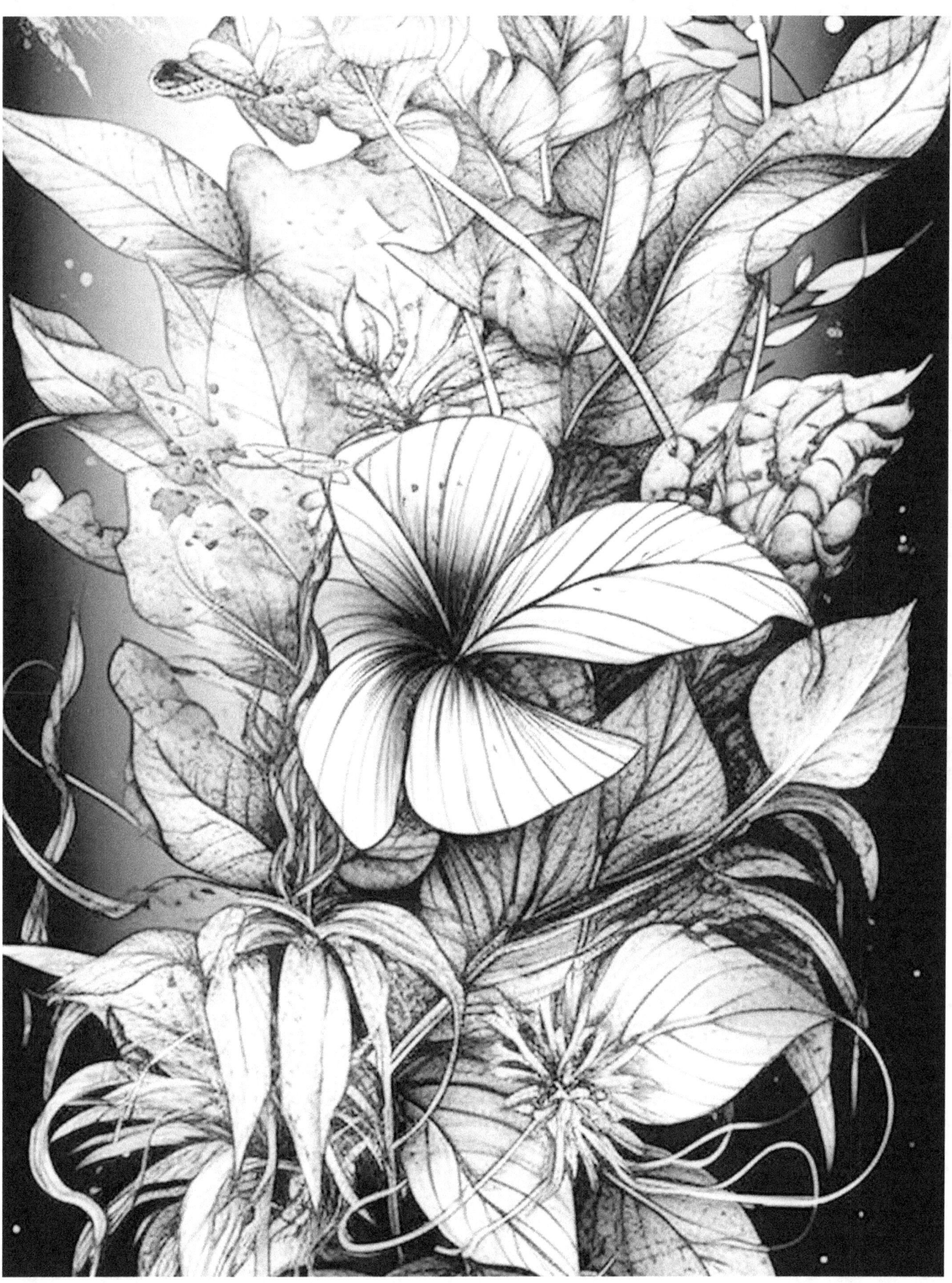

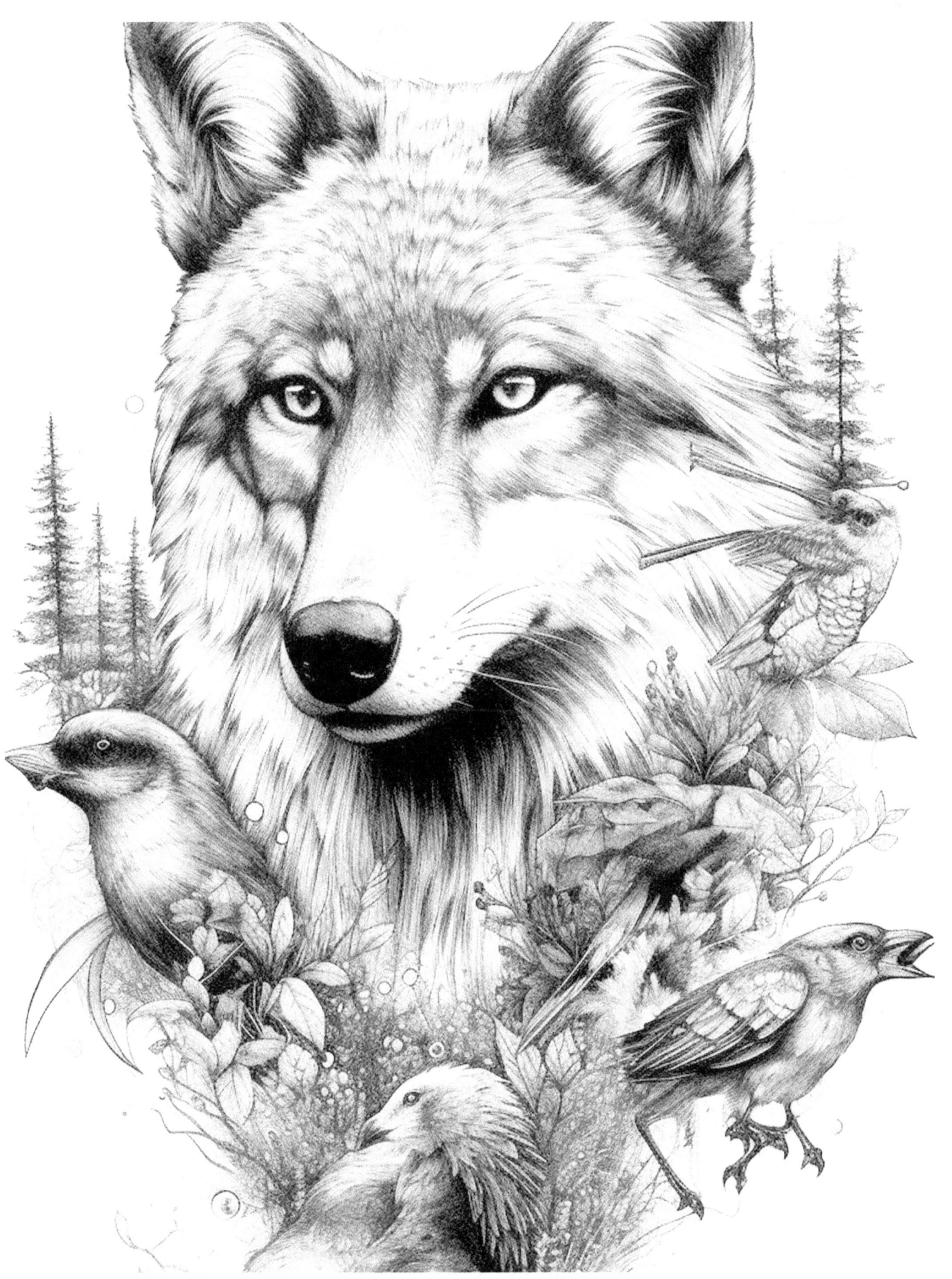

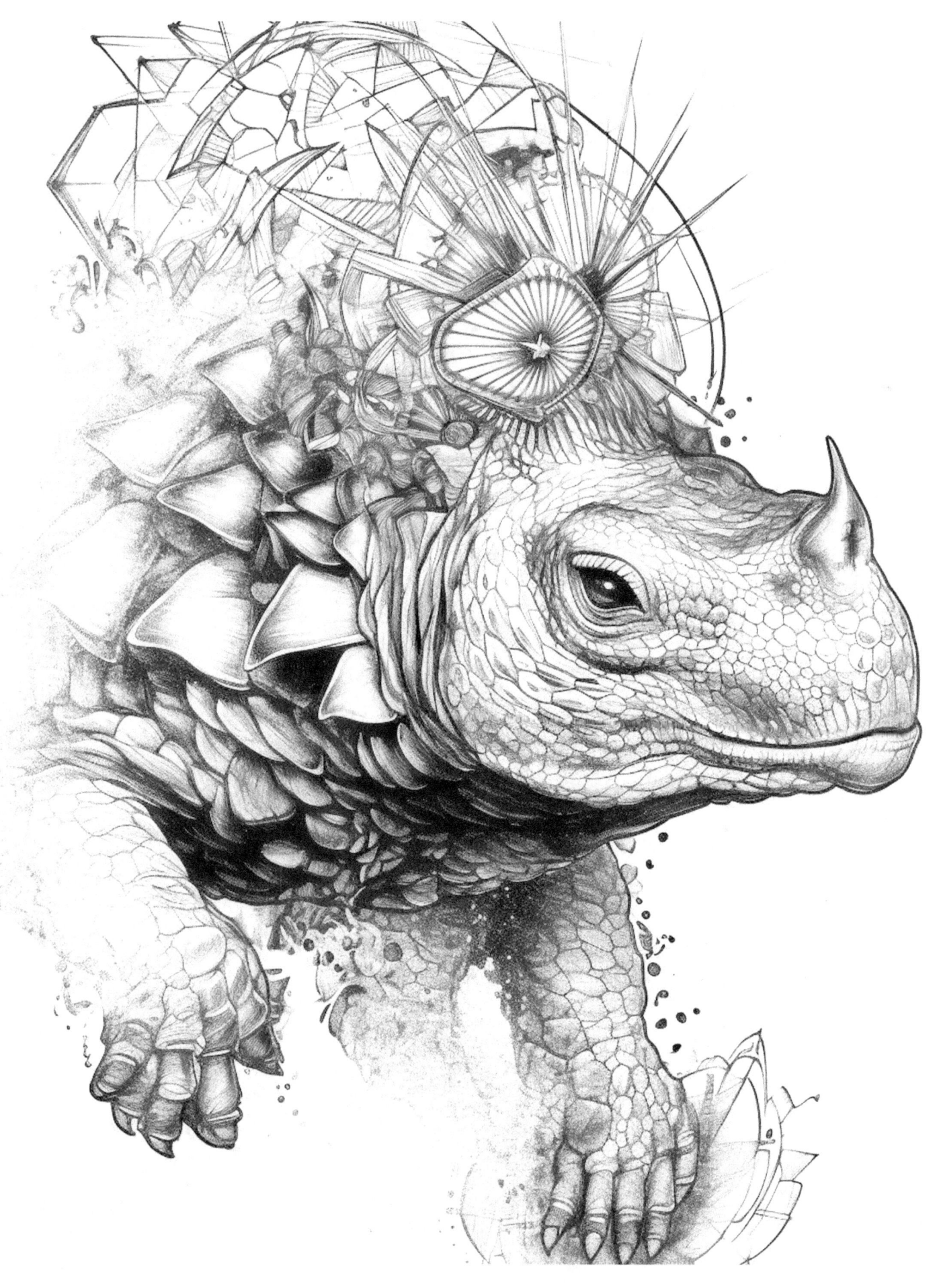

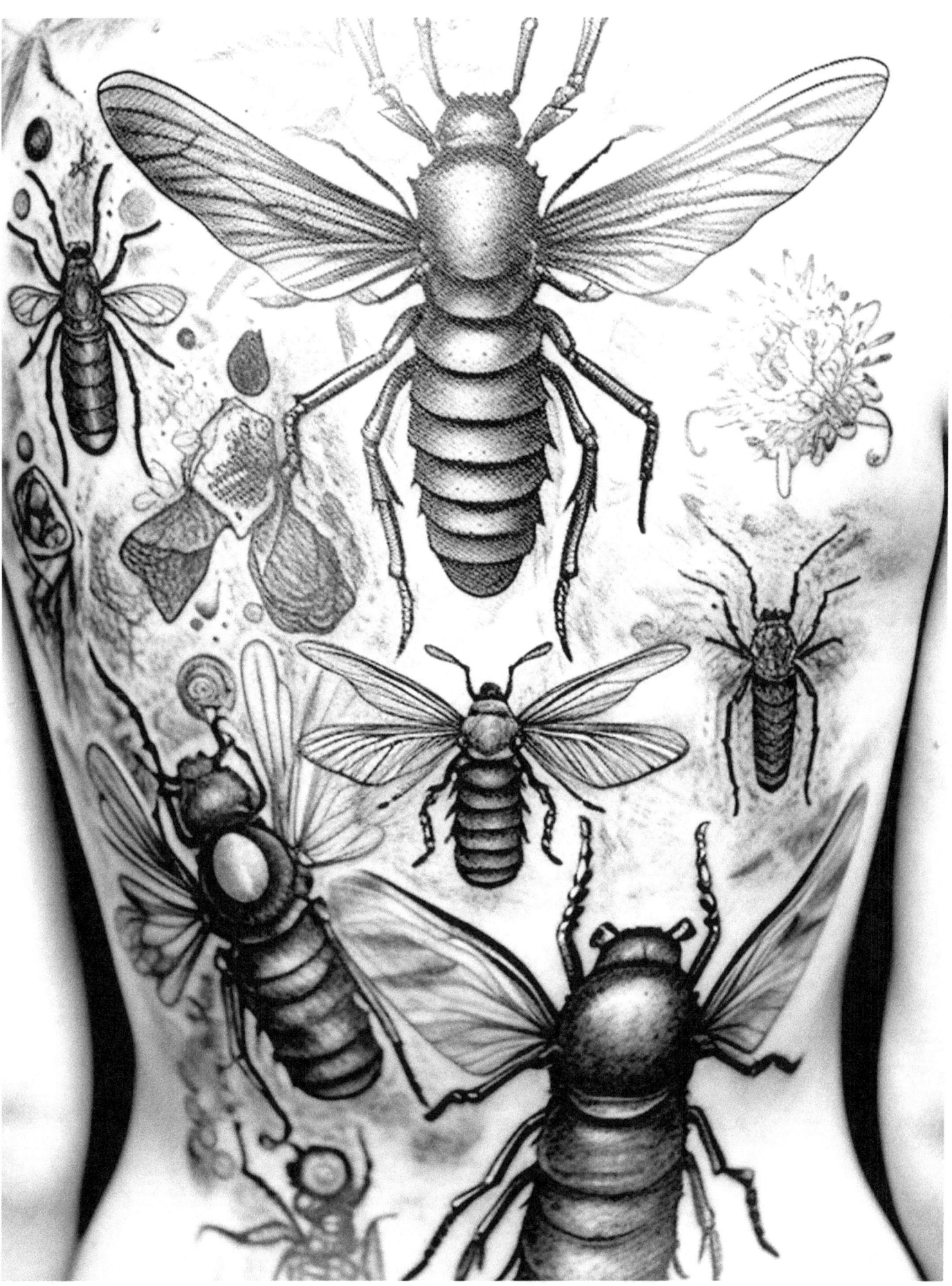

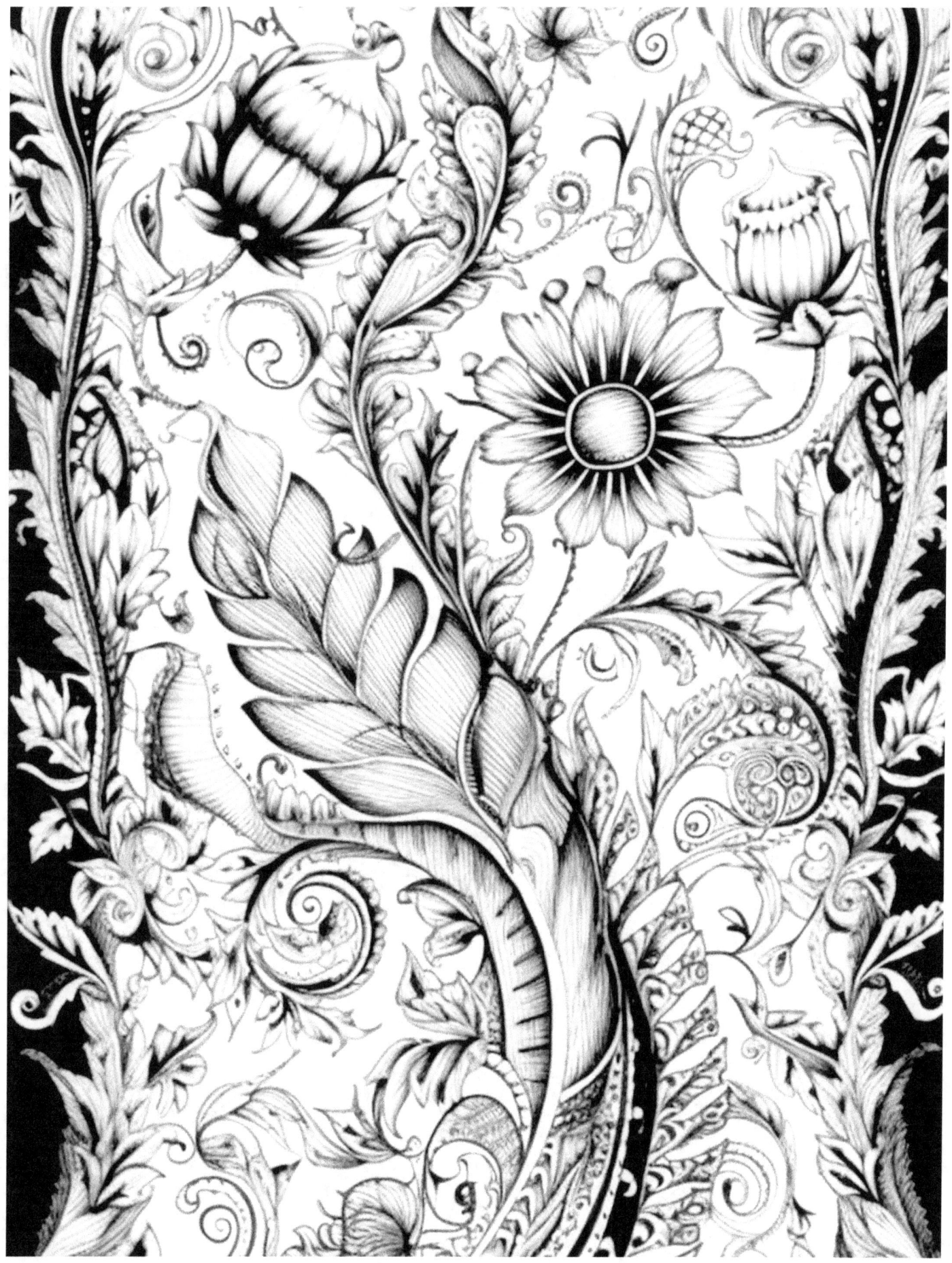

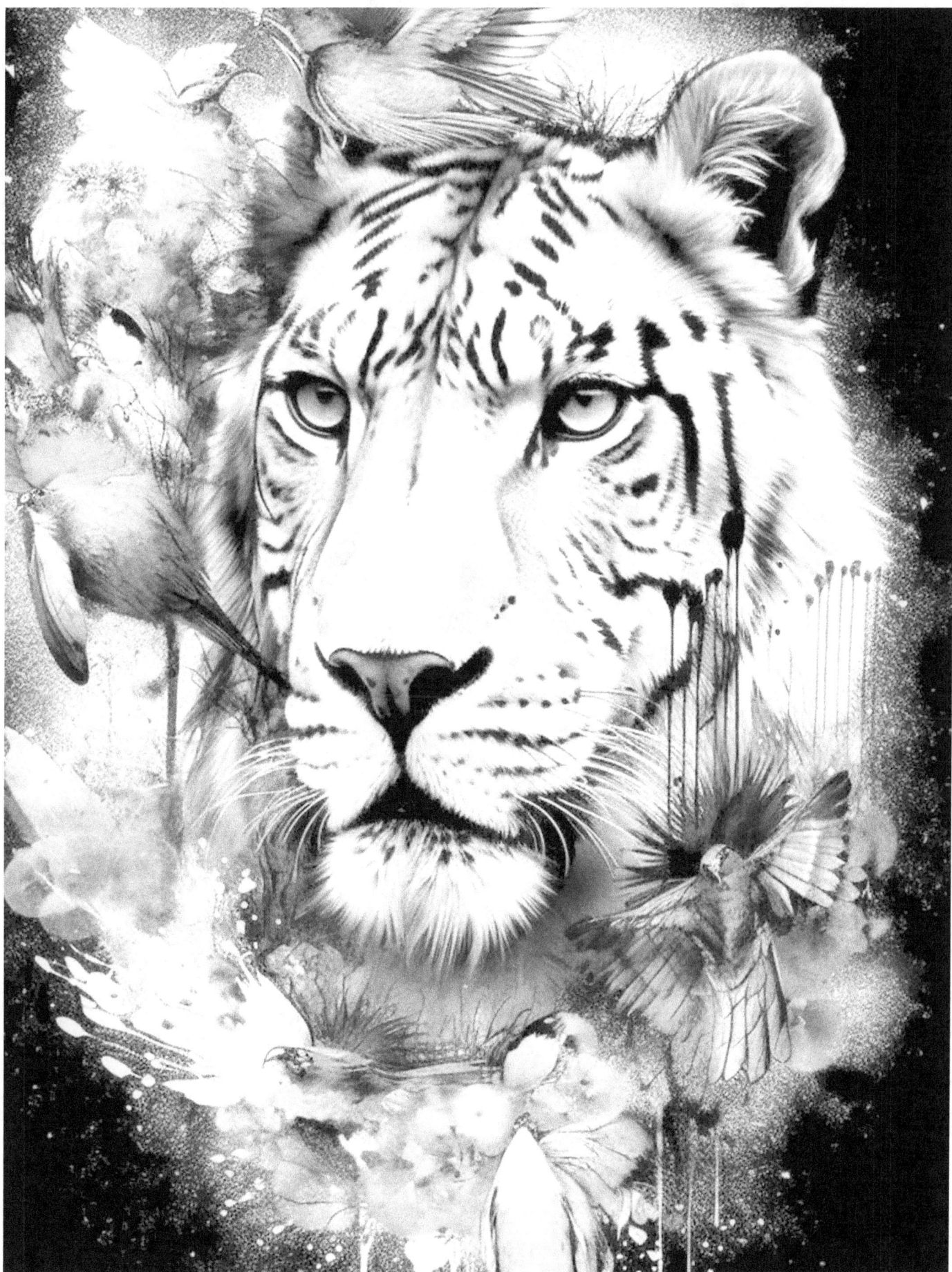

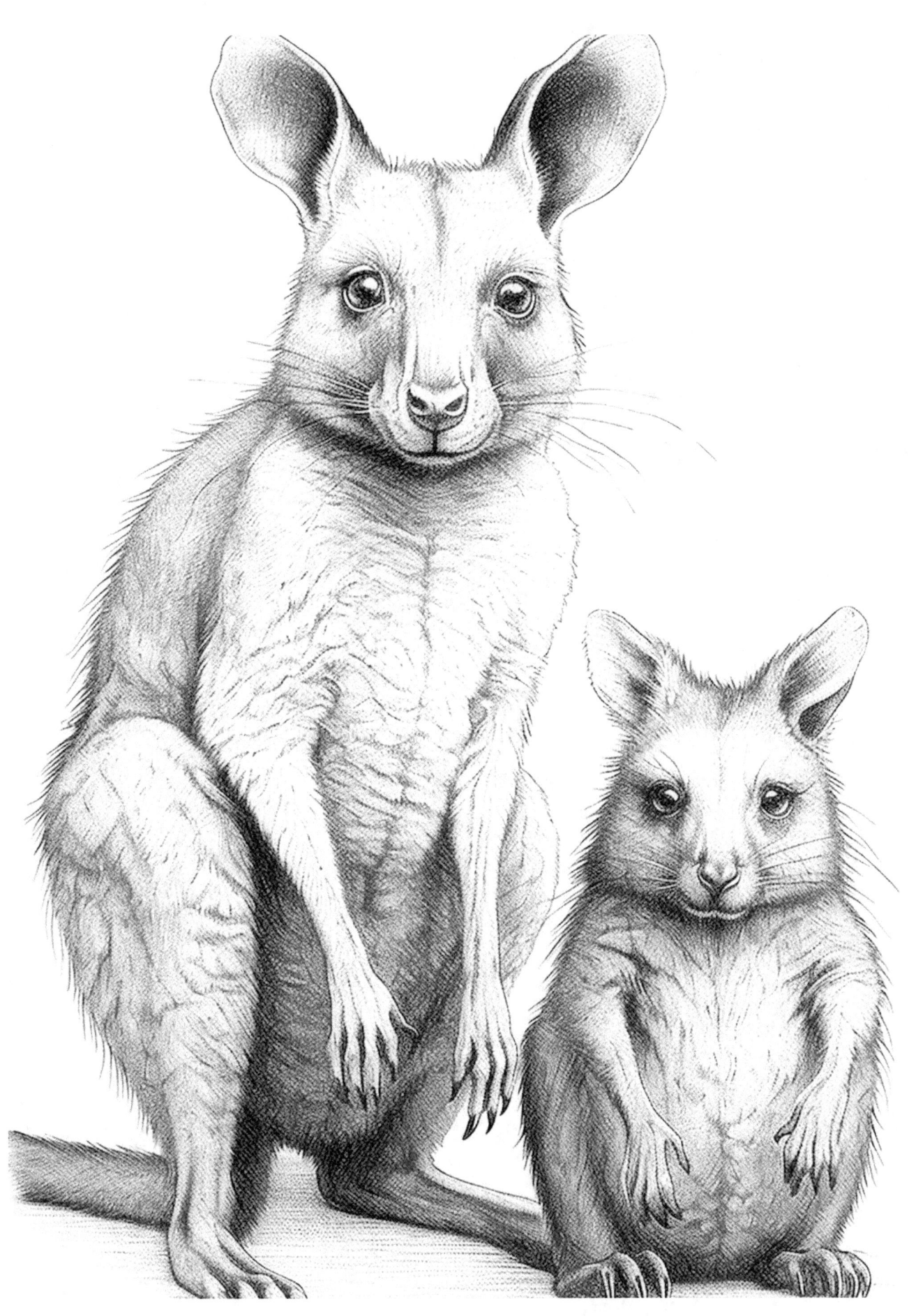

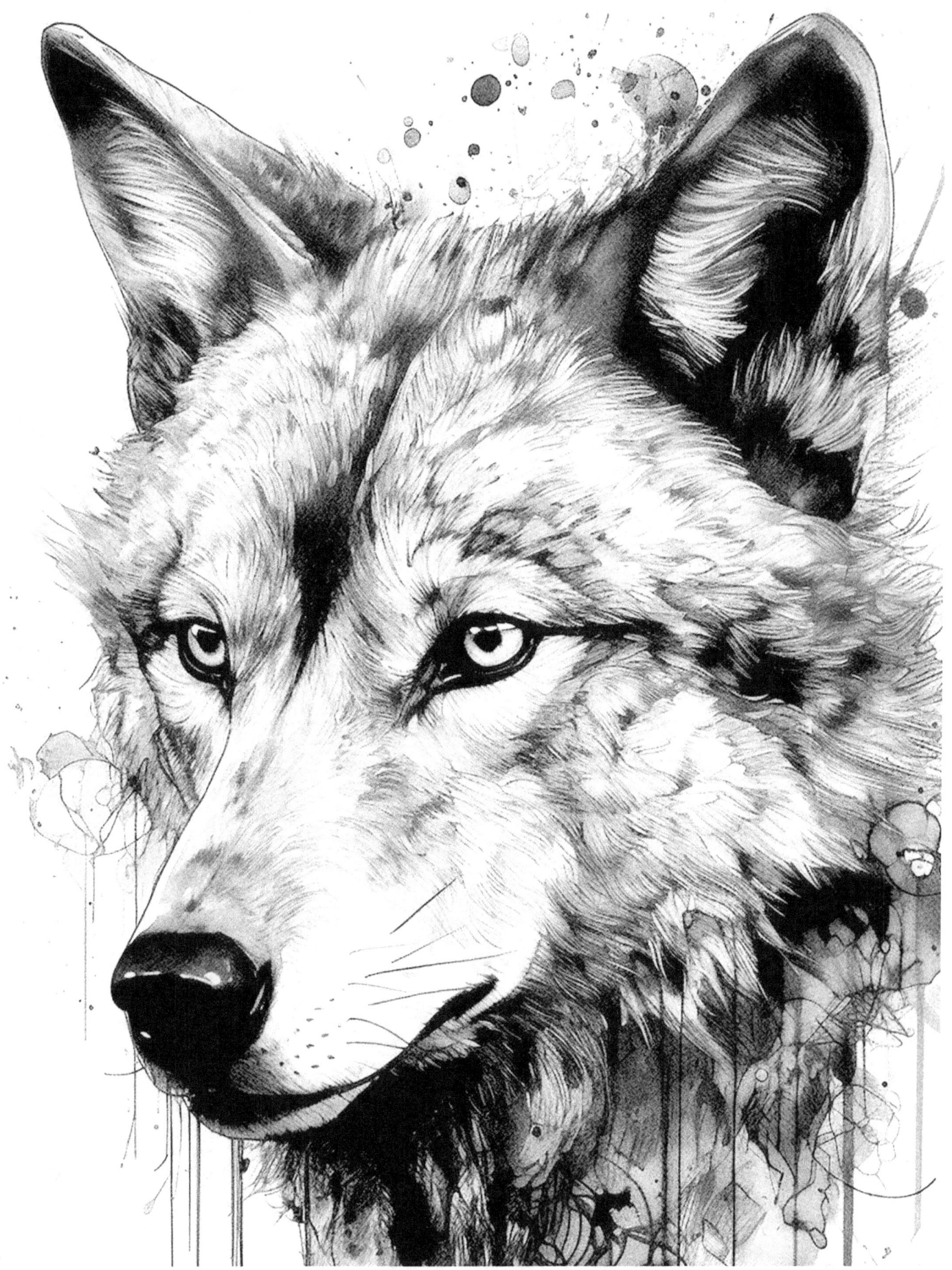

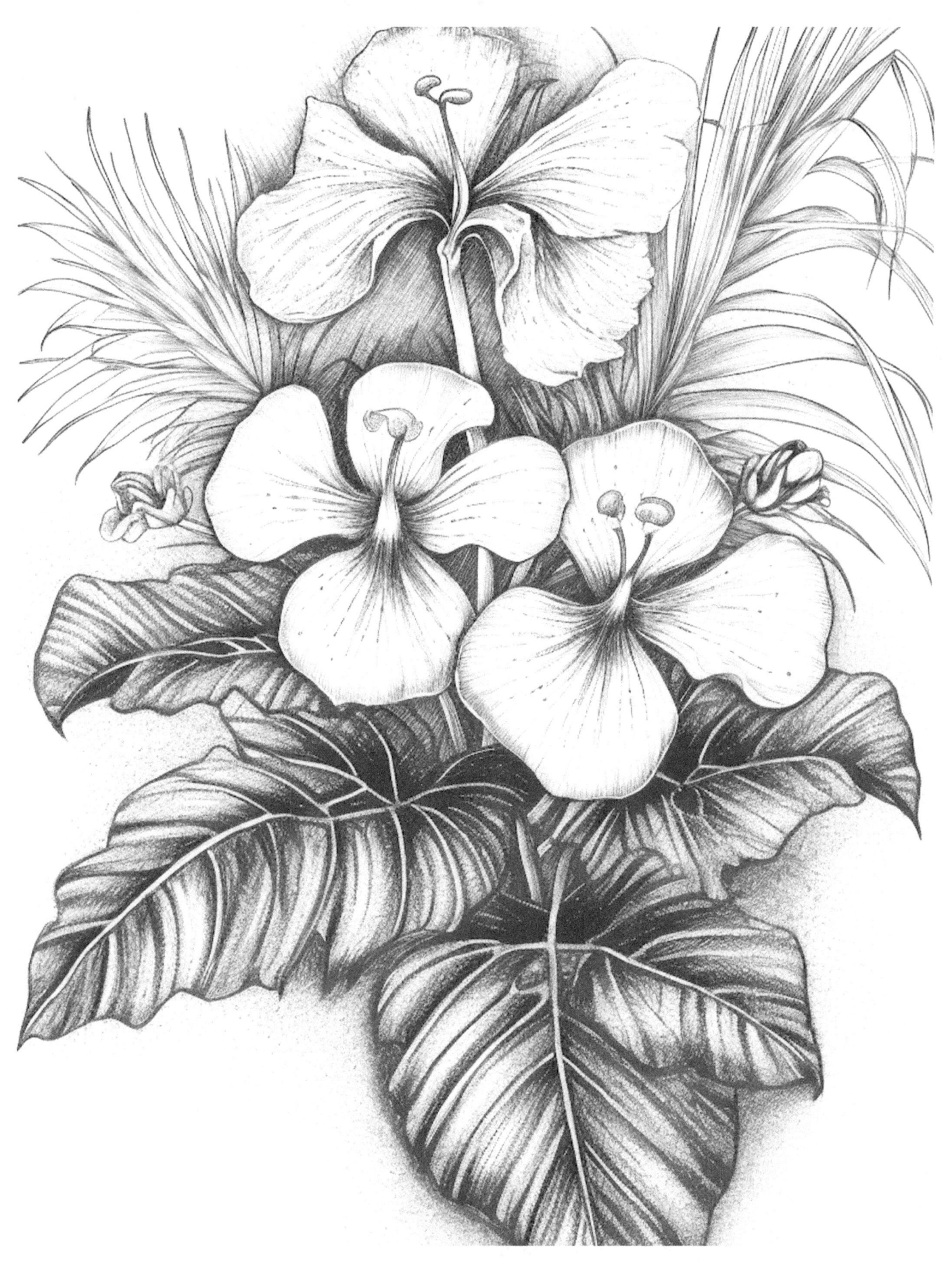

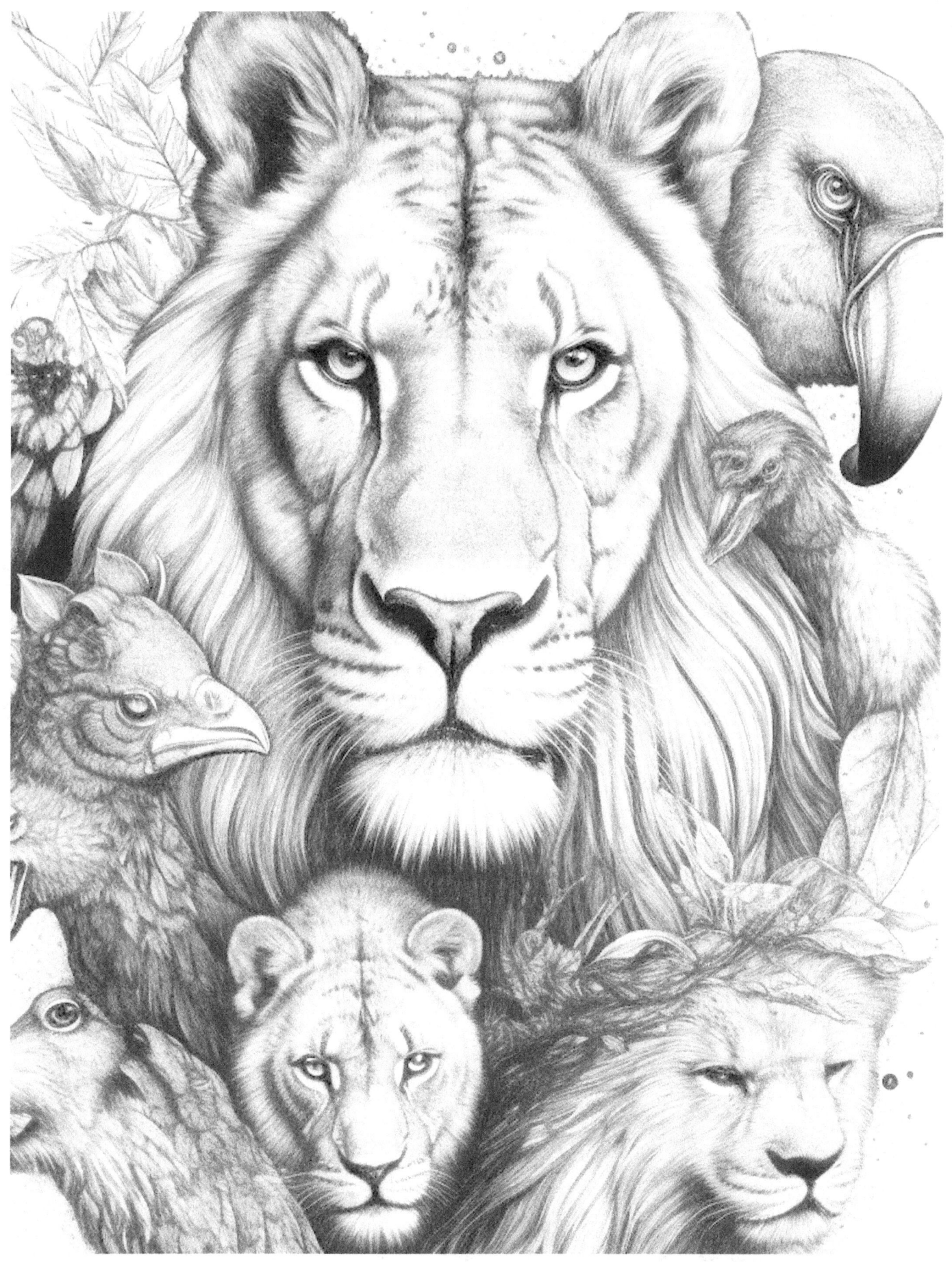

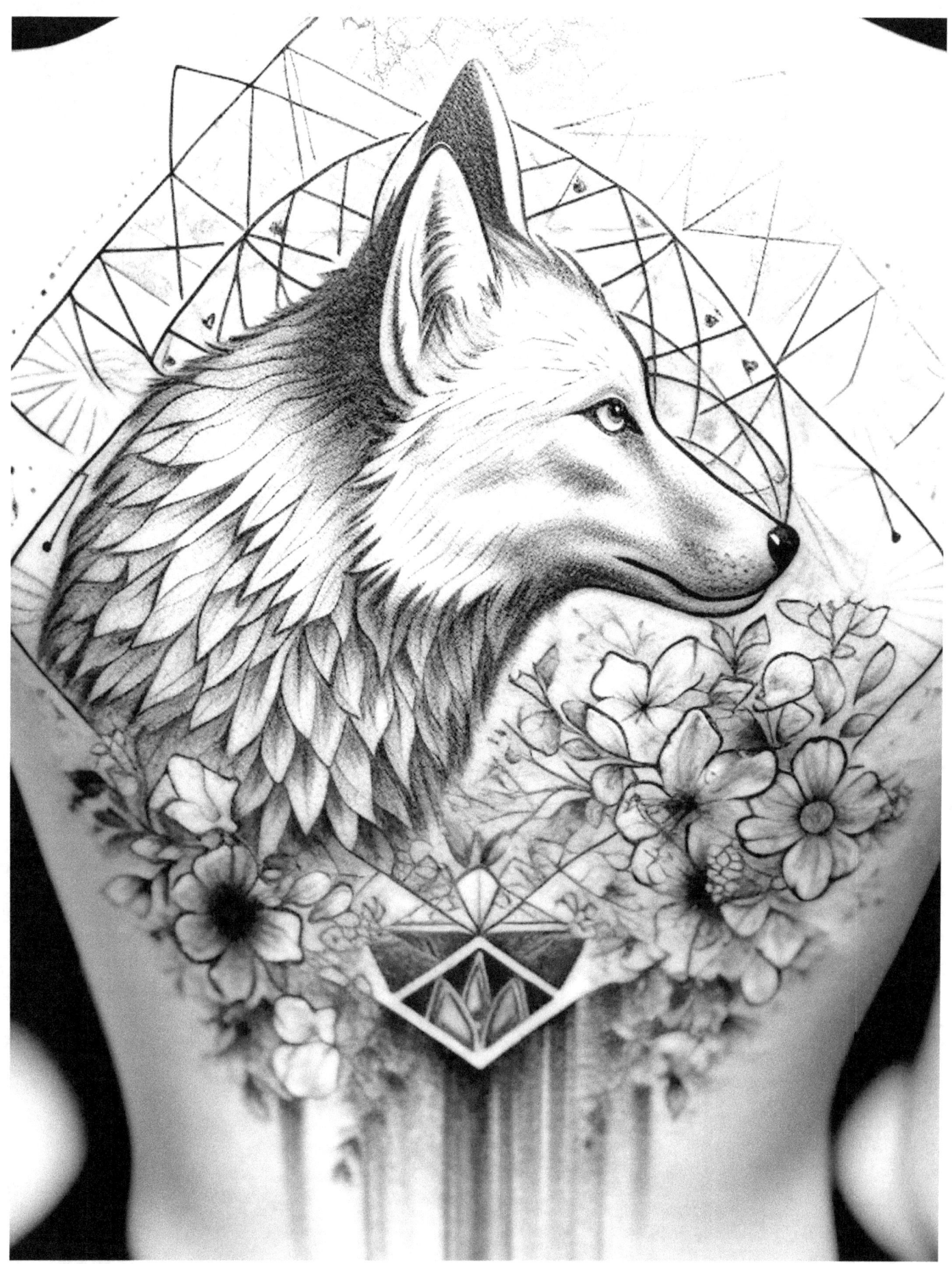

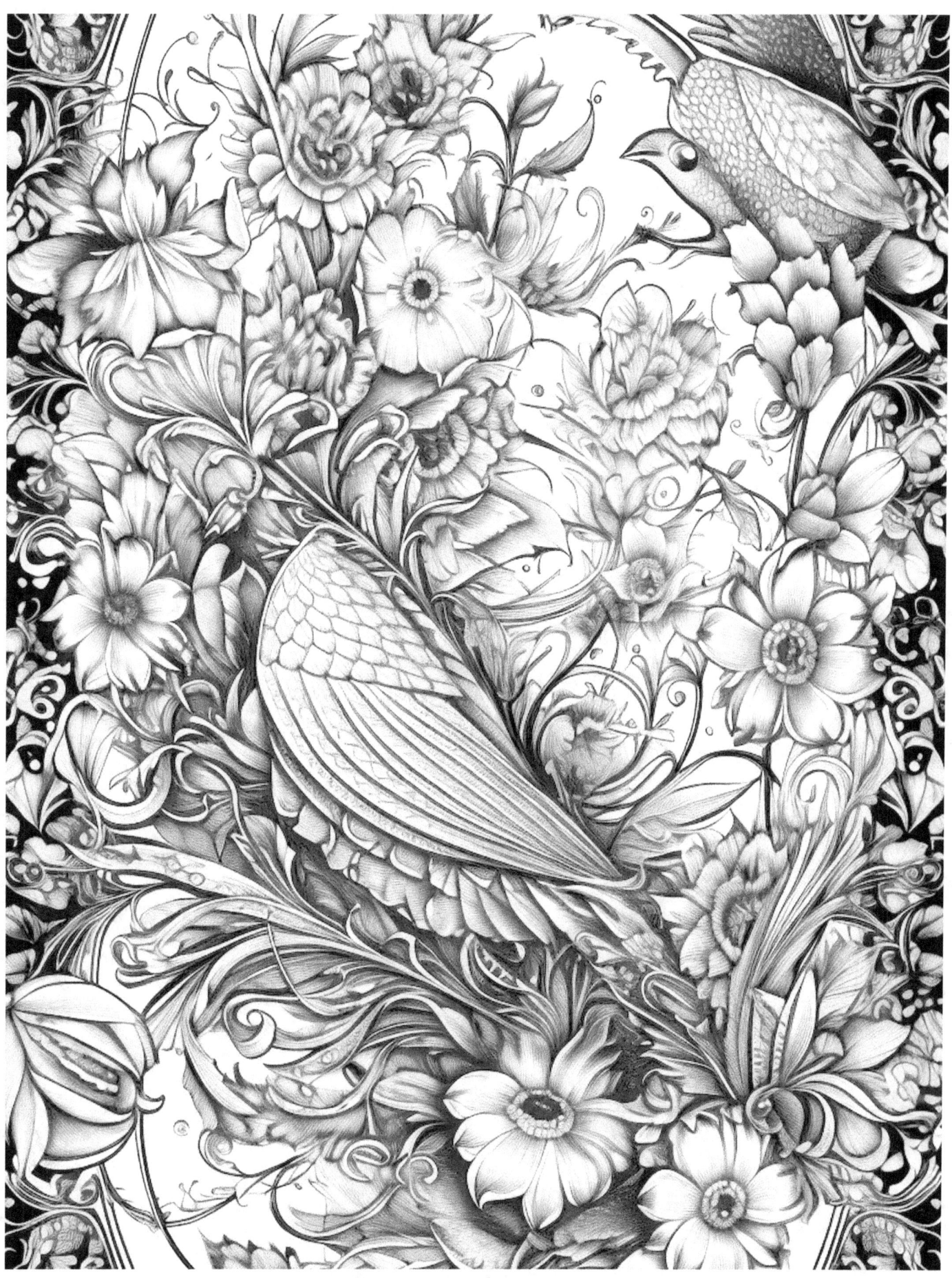

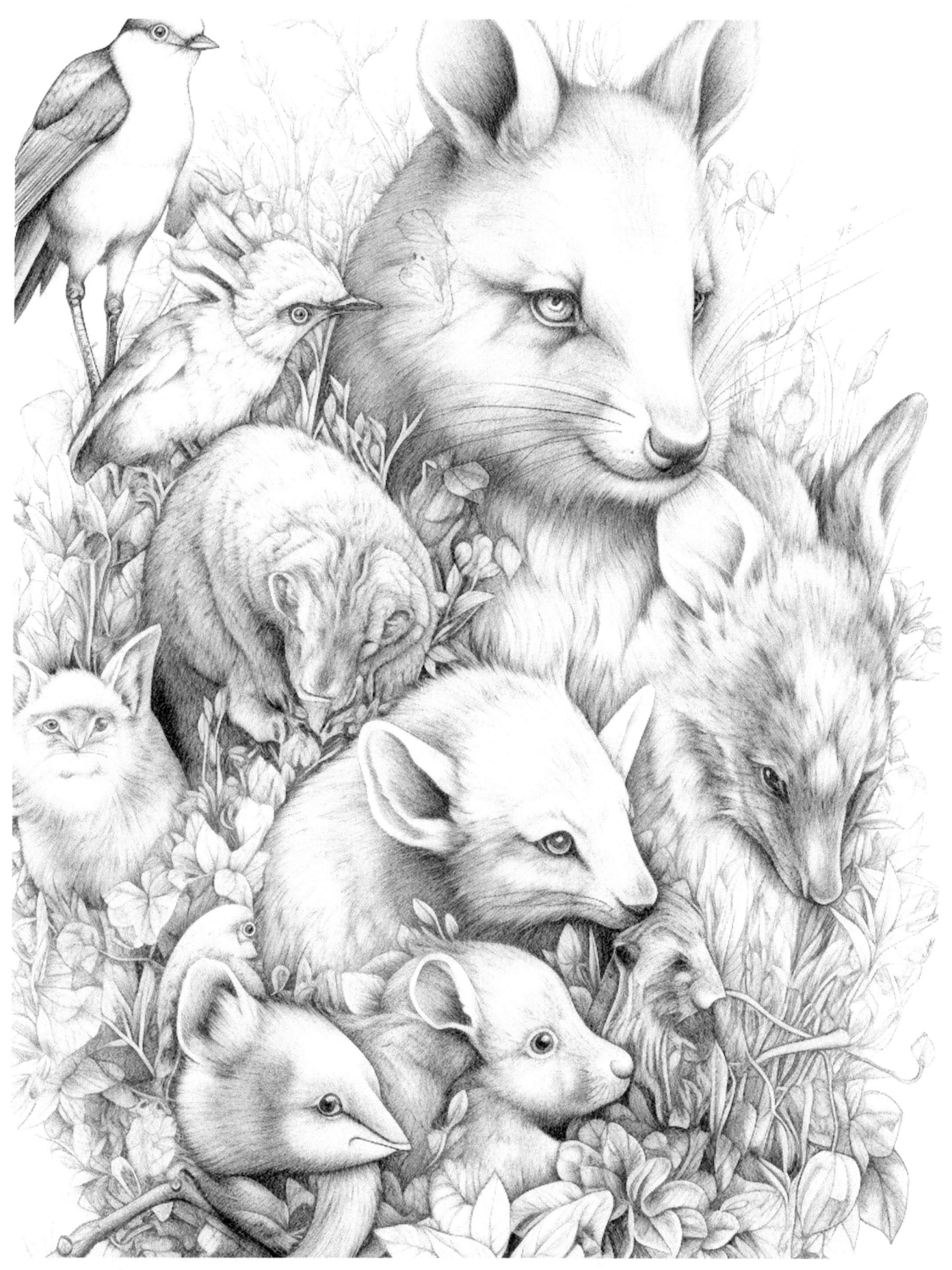

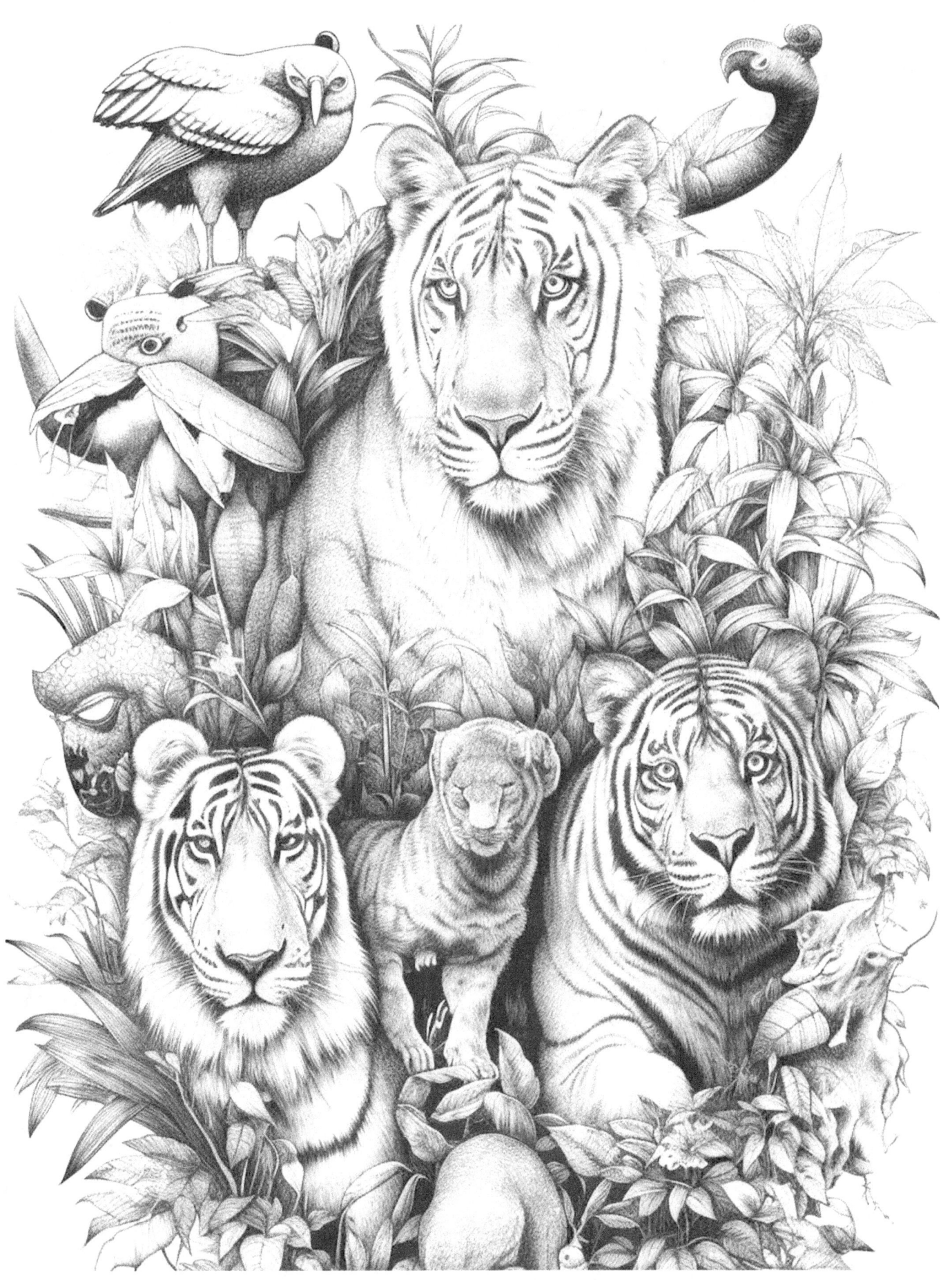

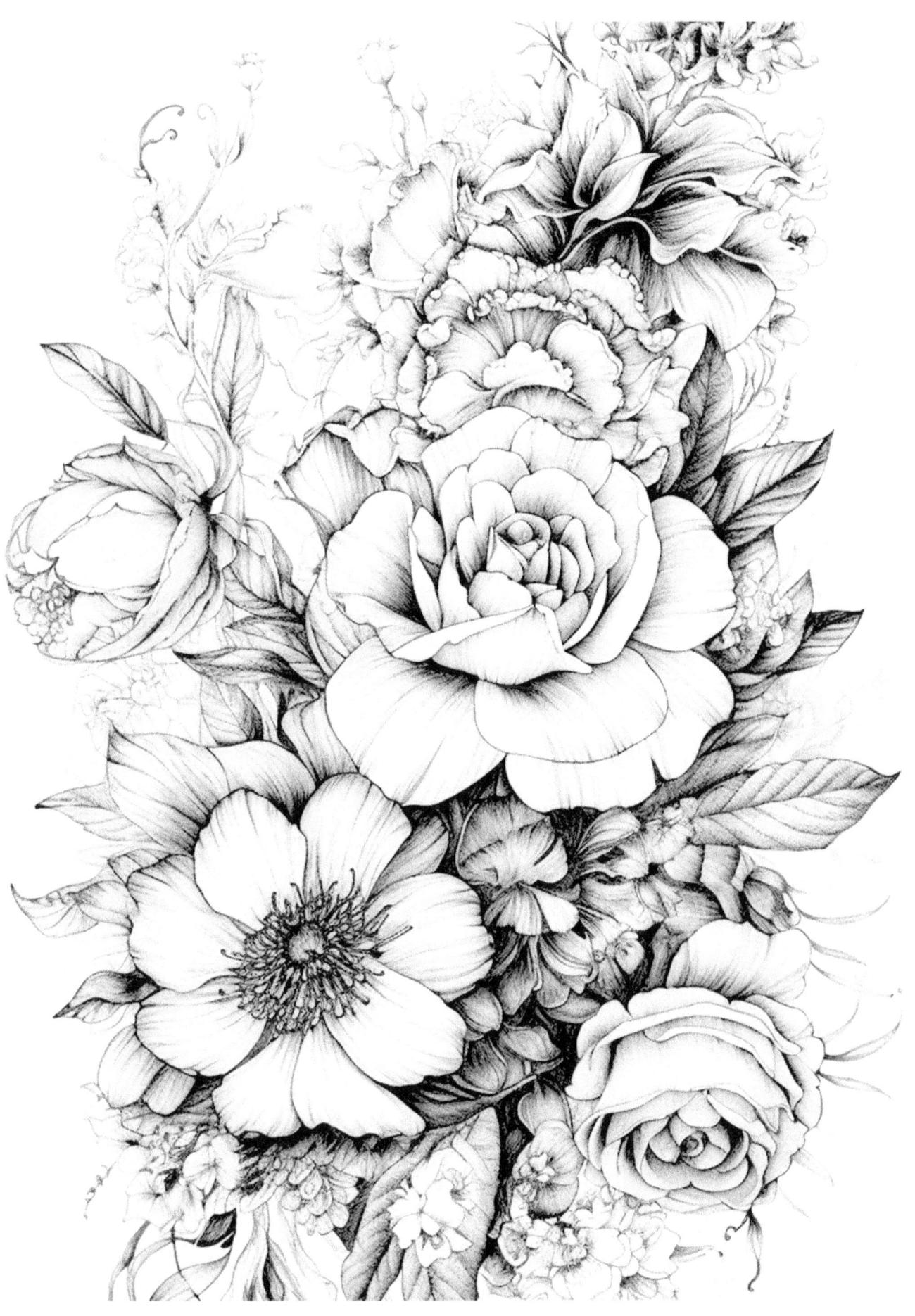

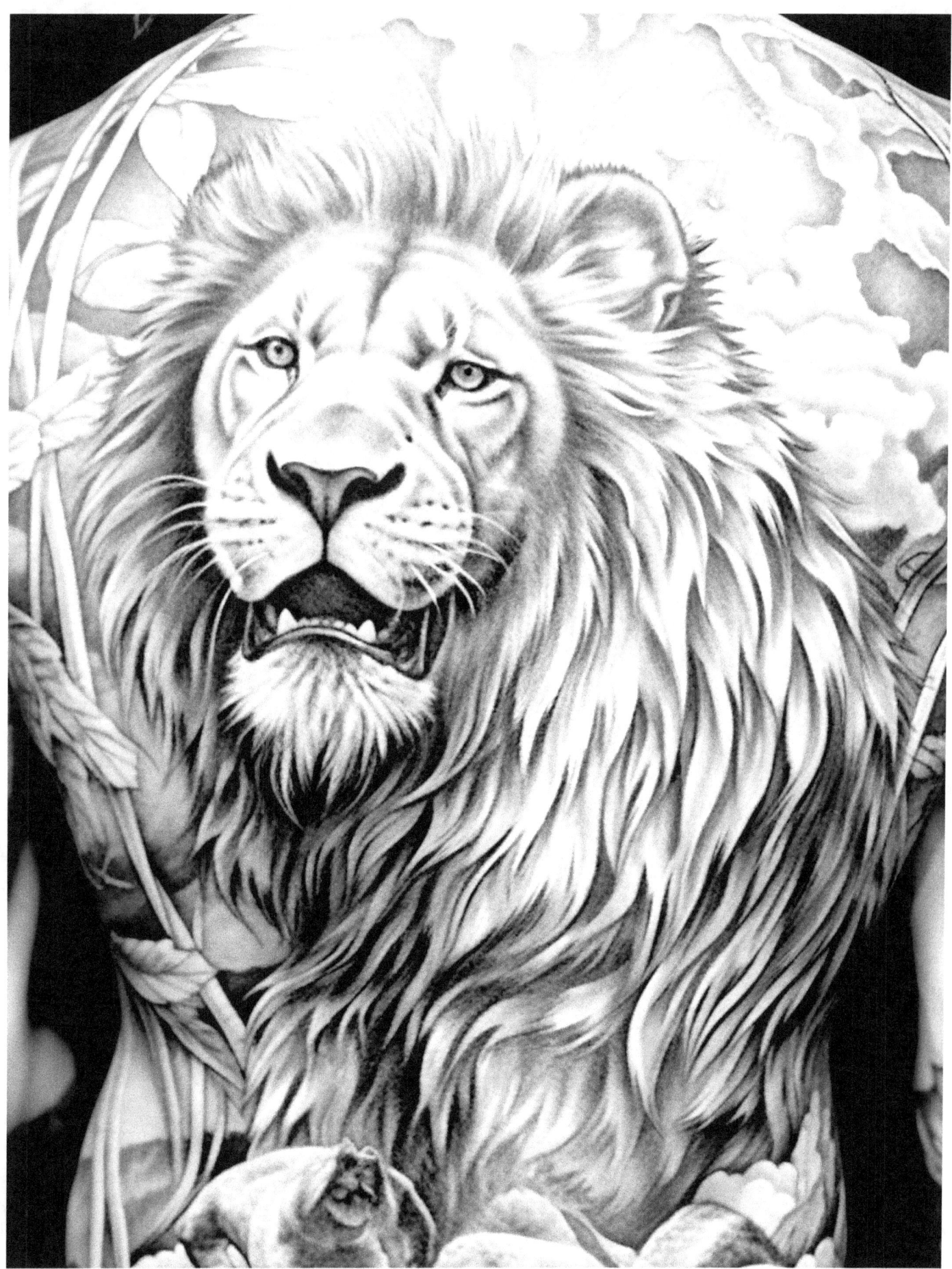

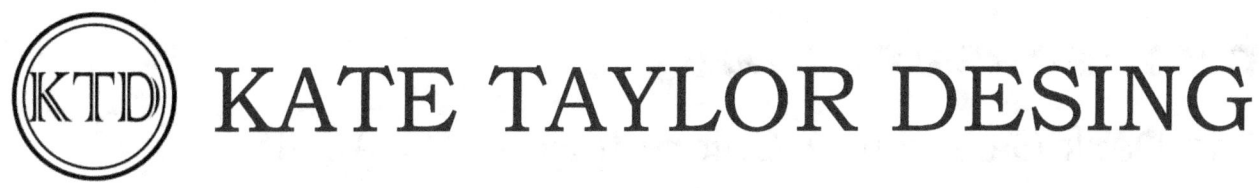

KTD KATE TAYLOR DESING

OTHER COLORING BOOKS:

MYSTICAL CREATURES

- A Dragon Coloring Book for Adults
- A Unicorn Coloring Book for Adults
- A Phoenix Coloring Book fo Adults
- A Fairy Coloring Book for Adults
- A Mermaid Coloring Book for Adults
- A Goblin Coloring Book for Adults
- A Gnome Coloring Book for Adults
- A Troll Coloring Book for Adults
- A Gryphon Coloring Book for Adults

VEHICLES

- American muscle cars coloring book for kids
- Supercars coloring book for kids
- Antique car coloring book for kids
- Jumbo cars coloring book for kids
- Motorcycle Coloring book for kids

THE HORRORS OF COLOR

- The Dark Carnival: A Coloring Book for Adult
- The Haunted Mansion: A Coloring Book for Adults
- The Curse of the Mummy: A Coloring Book for Adults
- Nightmare Bugs: A Coloring Book for Adults
- Dark Witchcraft: A Coloring Book for Adults
- The Spectral World: A Coloring Book for Adults
- Cemetery Chronicles: A Coloring Book for Adults
- Sinister Forest: A Coloring Book for Adults
- Vampire Dreams: A Coloring Book for Adults
- Horror coloring book

ARTISTIC ADVENTURES

- Surreal Escapes: A Coloring Book for Adults
- Cubist Explorations: A Coloring Book for Adults
- Impressionist Sensations: A Coloring Book for Adults
- Art Nouveau Revival: A Coloring Book for Adults
- Art Deco Magic: A Coloring Book for Adults
- Baroque Beauty: A Coloring Book for Adults
- Renaissance Reflections: A Coloring Book for Adults
- Neo Classical Nostalgia: A Coloring Book for Adults
- Romantic Visions: A Coloring Book for Adults
- Expressionist Inspiration: A Coloring Book for Adults

GEOMETRIC PATTERNS

- Geometric shapes and patterns coloring book
- Adult coloring book tessellations patterns
- Adult coloring book geometric patterns
- Adult coloring book circular patterns.
- 150 Mandala coloring book
- Wild Wonders: Animal Mandala Patterns
- Window to the Soul: A Stained Glass Coloring Book
- Enchanted Blossoms 1: A Floral Mandala Coloring Book
- Enchanted Blossoms 2: A Floral Mandala Coloring Book
- Oceanic Odyssey: A Seaside Mandala Coloring Book

WILD WEST TALES

- Pioneers and Settlers: A Western Coloring Book
- Gunslingers and Lawmen: A Western Coloring Book
- Frontier Towns: A Western Coloring Book
- Old West Architecture: A Coloring Book
- Untamed Horizons: A Western Scenery Coloring Book
- Rustic Portraits: A Coloring Book of Western Wildlife
- Valiant Women: A Coloring Book of Western Ladies
- Western Whirl: A Dance Hall and Entertainers Coloring Book

SCI-FI FANTASIES

- Alien Worlds: A Coloring Book for Adults

- Alien Encounters: A Coloring Book for Adults

- Robots and Cyborgs: A Coloring Book for Adults

- Space Transportation: A Coloring Book for Adults

- Cosmic Colonization: A Coloring Book for Adults

- Steampunk Revolution: A Coloring Book for Adults

- Cyberpunk Realm: A Coloring Book for Adults

- Dystopian Society: A Coloring Book for Adults

- Retro Futurism: A Coloring Book for Adults

- Biopunk Evolution: A Coloring Book for Adults

SKIN CANVAS DESIGNS

- Timeless Traditions: A cultural Tattoo Coloring Book

- Savage Tattoos: A Nature and Animal Coloring Book

QUOTES

- Inspirational quotes from the bible coloring book
- Money quotes coloring book
- Quotes for success coloring book
- Funny Mom Quotes and Patterns coloring book
- Motivational swear words coloring book

CHILDREN

- The Toddler Coloring Book
- Unicorn Coloring Book
- Dinosaur Coloring Book
- Mermaid Coloring Book
- Kawaii Friends Coloring Book

OTHER

- Flower coloring book
- Reverse coloring book

Love our coloring books? Subscribe to our newsletter for exclusive offers, new release updates, and a FREE bonus coloring page! Scan the QR code to sign up.

For more fantastic designs and exclusive content, visit our website: http://www.ktdesigndigital.com